Preventing and Detecting Employee Theft and Embezzlement

Preventing and Detecting Employee Theft and Embezzlement

A Practical Guide

STEPHEN PEDNEAULT

WILEY

John Wiley & Sons, Inc.

Published by John Wiley & Sons, Inc., Hoboken, New Jersey.

Published simultaneously in Canada.

Library of Congress Cataloging-in-Publication Data:

Pedneault, Stephen, 1966–
    Preventing and detecting employee theft and embezzlement: a practical guide/Stephen Pedneault.
        p. cm.
    Includes bibliographical references and index.
    ISBN 978-0-470-54571-3 (cloth)
    1. Employee theft—Prevention. 2. Employee theft. 3. Embezzlement—Prevention. 4. Embezzlement. 5. Employee crimes—Prevention. I. Title.
    HF5549.5.E43P43 2010
    658.3'8—dc22

                                                                2009054062

Printed in the United States of America

10 9 8 7 6 5 4 3 2 1

To all my clients, past, present, and future, who allow me to help guide them through the maze of money, piecing together financial puzzles during the good times and when things appear at their worst.

Contents

Preface   xiii

Acknowledgments   xvii

Introduction   xix

CHAPTER 1   Hiring the Right Employees   1

    Disclaimer   1
    Where Do You Start?   1
    Advice of Counsel   3
    Application Policy   3
    Due Diligence   5
    Personal Information   7
    Past Employment   8
    Education   9
    References   11
    Criminal and Civil History Checks   11
    Credit Checks   13
    Hiring Time   14
    Hiring the Right Employees: Considerations   17

CHAPTER 2   Know Your Employees   19

    Why Is Knowing Your Employees Important?   24
    Open Communications   25

What Should You Watch for in
Your Employees?   26
Know Your Employees: Considerations   29

CHAPTER 3   Sales, Cash Receipts, and Collections   31

Here's Where Everything Starts   31
Recording and Tracking Sales   32
Collections   44
Debit Memos and Other Adjustments   48
Accounts Receivable   52
Sales, Cash Receipts, and Collections:
Considerations   54

CHAPTER 4   Credit Card Sales, Transactions, and
Merchant Statements   59

Processing Sales   59
Reconciling Sales   61
Processing Refunds or Credits   61
Reviewing and Reconciling Refunds
or Credits   63
Reviewing and Reconciling the Merchant
Statement   67
Credit Card Sales, Transactions, and
Merchant Statements: Considerations   69

CHAPTER 5   Purchases, Cash Disbursements, Checks,
and Petty Cash   71

Purchases   75
Cash Disbursements/Checks   80
Unpaid Bills/Accounts Payable   84
Petty Cash   86
Purchases, Cash Disbursements, Checks,
and Petty Cash: Considerations   88

CHAPTER 6 Credit Cards and Debit Cards   91

    Credit Cards   94
    Debit Cards   96
    Credit Cards and Debit Cards:
      Considerations   99

CHAPTER 7 Employee Expense Reimbursement   103

    Expense Submission   104
    Where Are the Abuses?   106
    Payment Processing   109
    Employee Expense Reimbursement:
      Considerations   111

CHAPTER 8 Electronic Banking   115

    Traditional Banking (In-Person Deposits
      and Manual Check Writing)   115
    Check Processing and Clearing
      Changes   117
    Changes in Bank Deposits   120
    ATMs   121
    Online Banking   122
    What Can You Do?   123
    Electronic Banking: Considerations   132

CHAPTER 9 Payroll Processing   137

    Payroll Administration: Adding/Changing/
      Terminating   138
    Payroll Processing   142
    Payroll Tax Returns   149
    Payroll Processing: Considerations   151

CHAPTER 10   Inventory Issues and Controls   153

Prevention: Good News and Bad News   153
Retail Businesses: Items Available for Sale   153
All Businesses: Items for Use by Employees
   (Supplies, Tools, and Equipment)   166
Detection   166
Inventory Issues and Controls:
   Considerations   169

CHAPTER 11   Bank Statements, Canceled Checks, and
   Reconciliations   173

Bank Statements   177
Investment Account Statements   178
Canceled Checks   178
Bank Reconciliations   181
Bank Statements, Canceled Checks, and
   Reconciliations: Considerations   187

CHAPTER 12   Financial Reports   189

Generate Financial Reports Regularly   190
Why Is the Regular Review of Financial
   Reports So Important?   195
When to Consider Outside Advice
   and Assistance   196
Financial Reports: Considerations   202

CHAPTER 13   Safeguarding Your Bookkeeping or
   Accounting Systems   205

Manual Bookkeeping Systems   206
Computerized Bookkeeping and
   Accounting Systems   209
QuickBooks Users   222

Safeguarding Your Bookkeeping or
Accounting Systems: Considerations   224

CHAPTER 14 Prevention, Detection, and Insurance   227

Timing Is Everything   229
Adequacy of Coverage   230
Responsibilities for a Claim   230
Disclaimer   235
Prevention, Detection, and Insurance:
Considerations   236

CHAPTER 15 Your Response to an Identified or
Potential Issue   239

A Dreaded Day of Discovery   239
Due Diligence on the Discovery   243
What If It Appears to Be Fraud?   246
Your Response to an Identified or
Potential Issue: Considerations   249

*Appendix A: Embezzlement Controls for
Business Enterprises*   253

Appendix B: Who Was Lester Amos Pratt?   291

About the Author   295

Index   297

Preface

This book was inspired by a small business owner whose story follows in the introduction. He is referred to as Jeff, and in my more than 22 years of professional experience as a certified public accountant and certified fraud examiner, I have dealt with hundreds of small business owners similar to him. Not every owner was a victim of fraud or embezzlement, but many of them shared common traits. They were excellent in regard to the products they sold or the services they provided. They were very busy, working long hours to ensure their companies were, and remained, successful. They recognized their lack of financial knowledge, sophistication, or their busy schedules, so they hired someone else to handle the financial aspects of their business. They failed to implement proper controls and delegated too much of their bookkeeping and accounting to someone else. And in many cases, they fell victim to the individual they entrusted with the financial aspects of their businesses.

Jeff's case inspired me to seek out any resources that were available designed specifically with the small business owner in mind. I was looking for resources beyond generalized articles concerning preventing employee theft and embezzlement, but rather books or guides to identify specific steps and measures small business owners need to implement to better protect the finances of their businesses. Also, I wanted to find books or guides written for owners with varying degrees of financial background and experience, concepts, concerns, and recommendations that were easily understood and ready for implementation in most contexts. Translated using Jeff's terminology, these sources would tell me the things I should be concerned about as a small business owner with employees, and tell me what I would need to do to have the proper financial controls in place.

In my quest, I discovered a used book available online that described exactly what I was seeking. The price concerned me, a mere 12 cents, and I wondered how good a used book could be if it cost so little. It seemed as if someone was simply trying to get rid of it, and if they thought it was only worth 12 cents, then.... So I bought it. The shipping cost was 4,000 percent more than the book (still under $10). It was the best $10 I have ever spent. The book, *Embezzlement Controls for Business Enterprises*, was a great find—I discovered someone had written the very book I was seeking. The author had managed to cover the major areas of concern in just 31 pages, and he was right on with his recommendations. Many were applicable to situations I am involved with, even though the book was last published in 1952.

The author's name is Lester Amos Pratt, and throughout the writing of this book, I have done much research on his life. Lester's book has been reprinted with permission in Appendix A, with the exception of one chapter, and more about his life and accomplishments can be found in Appendix B.

The goal of this book is to deliver a readable, practical resource geared specifically to help very busy small business owners implement key controls and procedures to better protect themselves from employee theft and embezzlement. This book is designed to allow busy small business owners to read one chapter at a time and, using the checklists at the end of each chapter, begin to implement within their business the applicable measures provided, just as Jeff did, as told in the introduction.

Following a schedule of reading one chapter at a time and implementing associated changes within your business, a complete implementation covering all the financial areas would be limited only by the pace at which you read each chapter. If you complete one chapter each night—a realistic goal for many small business owners—you could accomplish a total evaluation of the financial policies and procedures within your business in less than two weeks. Regardless of the pace you follow, as long as you continue through each chapter and apply the information to your business, you will be better able to prevent and detect employee thefts and embezzlements.

Once completed, this book should serve as a guide to monitoring the financial policies and procedures within your business going forward. The discussions contained in the chapters are specific to small business settings yet general enough to be applicable in most contexts. In some cases more detailed and specific controls, policies, and procedures would likely be warranted. For this reason, this book and the information provided within it should not be held as absolute but rather used as a general guide.

Acknowledgments

To my family, who watched with eagerness as I completed writing this book—my third in less than a year—anxiously awaiting the return to normalcy in my evening and weekend schedules while patiently and quietly listing all the things I now need to address that I have neglected for the past year due mainly to my writing.

To all my friends, colleagues, and trusted advisors, who continue to stand by me, offering me invaluable insight and advice to allow me to make informed decisions. I value the relationships I have built with each of you and look forward to a long and successful journey enjoying our successes.

To Helen Koven, my friend, publicist, and literary agent, who thought getting a book published was a really good idea, having two books published in a year was a great idea, and completing three books in the same year meant we were just out of our minds. Thank you for all your help and support—clearly there is no way I could have done any of this without your guidance, experience, and expertise.

To Timothy Burgard, Andy Wheeler, Stacey Rivera, Todd Tedesco, Laura Cherkas, and all the folks at John Wiley & Sons, who extended me the opportunity to write three books within a year. I look forward to growing our relationship with future endeavors.

To the Association of Certified Fraud Examiners, the leading international organization on fraud that pioneered credentialing and training opportunities for fraud prevention and investigation professionals worldwide.

And to all the fraud professionals around the globe, preventing and investigating financial crimes of one kind or another. Although we may come from different backgrounds and work within different contexts, I believe we all share the same goals and commitments to promoting ethical and honest behavior with the guarantee of realistic consequences for crossing the line—even once.

Introduction

Acolleague called to let me know he had provided my name and contact information to someone who might need my help.

A week later I received the call. It was a Tuesday morning in December, and I was working in my office. It was the first time I had been at my desk in over a week. Things had been busy in the world of fraud, and much of my time was spent out in the field putting cases together. From an embezzlement perspective, things were definitely good for my business. As for the victims, it was just another sign of the sad state of our society. The holidays can cause an increase in people stealing, and that certainly was the case for the current year.

The caller, whom I will refer to as Jeff (not his real name), said he was given my name by his accountant, a colleague of mine. He said he thought he had a problem within his business and wanted to meet as soon as possible. I asked him how urgent our meeting needed to be, and he asked me what I was doing that morning. Sensing the anxiety in his voice, I asked him if he had his morning coffee. He said he had a cup earlier but could use another. I offered to meet him and listen while he told me a little about what was happening.

I asked him where he wanted to meet, and he said somewhere where the meeting would not look suspicious. I told him I was dressed casually that day and that meeting me at a coffee shop could look pretty innocent. He said he had many customers in town and is recognized by someone almost every-where he goes. He suggested we meet at a doughnut shop just outside the center of town. I agreed and asked how I would recognize him. He said he would be driving a commercial van with the name of his business on the sides, and provided me with the business name. I told him I was on my way; it was a 10-minute drive for me at best. I told him the make and color of my car and where I would be parked in the lot.

I arrived first and backed into a spot, watching for a com-mercial van to pull in. Within a minute or so the van arrived. I watched as the driver spotted my car and drove over to park next to me. He waved and rolled down his window. I asked him if we were going to meet inside, and he said he would prefer to meet in his van to avoid being recognized. I grabbed my pad and pen, and put them on the passenger seat of his van. I asked him if he wanted a coffee, and he said he was all set. I told him I wanted to get something and walked into the shop. I bought an apple juice and a chocolate doughnut, then headed back to the van.

As I took the cap off my juice, I asked Jeff to tell me what was happening and why we needed to meet.

He started by telling me that he owned a local service com-pany, and had owned it for the past ten years or so. He had a partner who owned a small piece of the business; Jeff owned the majority of the company. Both he and his partner were employ-ees of the business; he ran the service end of things while his partner was responsible for the finances. Jeff said that recently, as he reviewed financial records and documents, he noticed activity and transactions that were not authorized. One example was his partner charging gas on the company's credit cards. Another example was his partner providing himself with an increase in compensation. Jeff said neither of these actions were approved or authorized by him. He said the worst thing he had discovered was that there were undeposited customer checks sitting in his partner's desk waiting to be processed. While that may not be a bad thing by itself, his partner was complaining there was insufficient cash in the business to purchase new equipment that Jeff wanted in the service area. He said he had begun looking further into the finances but knew nothing about finances, let alone the accounting and bookkeeping for the business. His partner handled all aspects of those areas, including maintaining the computer systems and files.

It didn't take me long to eat the doughnut, and by then I was ready to start asking some questions and taking some notes. Starting mainly with background information, I began to get a picture of the business environment. I asked if he thought his partner was aware that Jeff was looking into financial areas of the business, something that he had never done before. He said he didn't think his partner was aware of anything and that he had been very careful to put things back exactly where he had found them and to leave as much undisturbed as possible. His partner hadn't mentioned anything to him about his actions. He also said everyone was acting as they always did—business as usual. I asked him how much he found in undeposited checks; he replied that the customer checks he found totaled over $100,000.

I asked if he ever ran an accounts receivable report or had any sense of how much customers owed to the business. He said that too was an interesting question. He said his partner was always late in invoicing customers after work was completed, sometimes months later, and in some cases he thought the work was never invoiced. He also said he saw one accounts receivable report that included large balances well over 120 days old. In his line of business, his customers typically get invoiced once the service has been completed and pay within 30 days. He had no explanation why the billing to certain customers took so long and why their balances were so old.

As I listened to Jeff's story, I pretty much figured his partner was committing some type of cash receipts fraud, quite possibly lapping (where customer payments are diverted by the employee and later payments from other customers are used to cover the diverted payments). This could explain the large outstanding balances and the undeposited payments sitting in Jeff's partner's drawer. However, the increase in pay and the charged fuel purchases made me believe there was a lot more happening within the business and that the customer payments were only part of the scheme.

Jeff said his main concern was the continuity of his business and that if a theft was occurring, any investigation within the company could not interrupt the servicing of his customers. I asked him to describe all the areas of responsibilities of his partner and any assistants in any financial areas of the business. Jeff described just what I had expected: His partner was in charge of all the financial areas of the business, beginning to end, with no internal controls and no segregation of duties. Jeff also described a newly created position, an assistant to his partner, a position his partner adamantly tried to prevent being created. He said the individual currently working in that position had been there only a few months.

I asked Jeff to describe any financial roles he had in the business, and as I expected, he had few to none. Jeff confessed that he was great in the service area, working with his service employees and with customers, and was also responsible for completing bids for new work. However, when it came to the finances, he didn't have much time left over, and although he owned the majority of the business, he left the finances to his partner to manage.

Jeff also stated he wouldn't even know where to start with establishing internal controls or understanding the finances of the business, and would look to someone like me to help him identify what things he should be doing as the majority owner of his company.

Over the next hour or so we hashed out a plan on how to approach the issues, conscious of his primary goal of business continuity, and I provided him with the names of a few attorneys I thought he should consider getting involved for legal guidance.

Within a week we met again at the law office of the attorney he contacted and reviewed the issues and the plan to ensure all legal aspects were covered.

Two weeks later the plan was executed. In the course of a few short days, Jeff had taken control of both his company and the situation, and business continuity was unaffected.

It was during the first day at the company that I told Jeff he would need to make some immediate changes within his business and implement procedural changes to begin establishing internal controls over the financial aspects of the company. Jeff handed me a pad and pen, and told me to create a checklist of all the things I thought he needed to do. I told him I could type them up and bring them in the morning, but he insisted that I simply write them out so he could start implementing them as early as that night.

He said he had a business to run and his area of expertise was strictly in the service field. He said that I clearly knew what was needed to turn things around quickly to provide him the necessary control, and that he would execute whatever I wrote on my list. He said he simply didn't have time in his day to have meetings or read memos, but if provided a list with specific steps to implement, he could get those done.

I wrote out three pages of things he needed to change or implement. After I had completed it in the early evening hours of that first day, Jeff made a copy and kept the originals. He then took out a highlighter and asked me which measures he needed to implement immediately, meaning first thing tomorrow morning. I went through the list and pointed them out. He said once he had all the service staff out on their assignments for the day, he would work down the list and get as many done as practical by the end of the day.

By the end of day two Jeff reported back that he had completed all but one item on the list; the work had taken most of his day. He said he was added to the bank accounts, his partner was removed from all the bank accounts, the customer remittance address was changed to ensure he had sole control over all future customer payments, and so on.

■ ■ ■

In this case I was able to use my experience and expertise to have an immediate and direct impact on Jeff's business, as I have with many other businesses. While I enjoy these projects and interactions with business owners, I find myself drawing on my experience and creativity for each and every engagement, with no documented guide applicable to a typical small business environment. Such guidance would help me ensure that I cover all aspects of each business every time in a consistent manner and would provide me with documentation I could leave with business owners at the end of an engagement to allow them to monitor and modify their policies and procedures in response to changes in their businesses.

From implementing prudent hiring policies and practices through collecting receipts, making deposits, writing checks, paying employees, and evaluating the adequacy of insurance coverage, this book covers the major financial areas commonly found in most small businesses and provides the owners with practical information and recommendations applicable to their business environments to prevent and detect instances of employee theft and embezzlement.

It all starts with hiring the right people, which is what follows in Chapter 1.

CHAPTER 1

Hiring the Right Employees

Disclaimer

As I begin discussing the importance of sound hiring practices, I want to highlight that I am not an attorney and by no means am I providing you with legal advice. In my opinion nothing replaces the advice of counsel based on their experience and expertise. The discussions that follow are based solely on my personal experiences during my more than 22 years of working with clients and counsel to prevent and resolve a wide range of employment-related issues, many of which stem from some type of theft or embezzlement of assets, money, proprietary information, or a combination of all three.

Where Do You Start?

The first line of defense against employee fraud and embezzlement is to hire the most qualified and most trustworthy individuals to work in your business, especially those employees who will have access to your company's finances. The problem is, in this day and age, that is easier said than done. There are so many laws and rules geared toward protecting potential employees from improper hiring practices that even when you perform proper due diligence with your candidates, you will be limited in what you can ask, where you can gain information, and how you can use the information you do obtain in your hiring decision. Contacting past employers will likely yield you no more than the individual's date of hire, date of termination, and whether the individual is eligible for rehire. In my experience, as much as the past employer would love to tell the next potential employer more of the details, especially if the individual was terminated for something like stealing, the past employer was advised by counsel to limit responses in order to minimize potential litigation brought by the terminated individual. Furthermore, if by chance the past employer did provide such details, the terminated individual likely has a right to know what information was provided and would be allowed an opportunity to provide a response. As with any other information obtained, you may find yourself defending a claim by a candidate and be forced to show how the information you received impacted your hiring decision. In my opinion, the deck is stacked against small business owners trying to create job opportunities while also trying to ensure that they don't hire someone who could negatively impact their business.

Often small business owners rely on referrals and references from colleagues and other known business associates. While these referrals should carry much weight, you would be wise to still perform an independent due diligence on the referred individual to ensure that the potential employee is qualified and trustworthy. Here's why. In one of my recent cases, it was discovered that the business manager was stealing from the business. This man had been strongly recommended by a vendor close to the business owners, who hired him, relying mainly on that recommendation. The same vendor was also serving other competing businesses within the same industry, and once the business manager was terminated from the company for stealing, he landed his next job at one of the competitors not far away. It is believed the business manager landed that next position due to the vendor's recommendations to the next company.

No reference calls were received from the competing business prior to hiring the business manager.

Advice of Counsel

As I mentioned earlier, nothing replaces the advice of counsel. This is what I recommend to every client I meet: If you envision having employees in your business, you should establish a relationship with an attorney who specializes in labor laws right from the inception of the business. Counsel's insight into how policies and procedures should be established will prove invaluable. If an attorney is involved in the design and implementation of your employment policies and procedures, he or she will be prepared to defend any labor actions brought against you and your company. The initial and ongoing investment you make with counsel will pay dividends should you ever find yourself defending a pre-employment or employment claim.

The caveat is that once the policies and procedures have been established and implemented, they need to be followed every time. The best defense regarding many labor issues is strict adherence to established policies and procedures and detailed documentation. The better a file is documented, the better a claim against you can be defended. I cannot overemphasize the need for adequate documentation.

Application Policy

Your company, regardless of its size, should have, at minimum, basic written policies and procedures regarding hiring and maintaining employees. You should have an established set of information you require from each candidate when filling job openings. The application you require every candidate to complete should be comprehensive and, as stated, should be reviewed by counsel to ensure completeness and adherence to hiring laws. All applications should be retained for a period of time, even after a successful hire, so in the event a candidate who didn't get hired brings about a claim for improper hiring practices, you have retained the details in your files for your defense.

In addition, clearly stated somewhere on the application should be your policy regarding a candidate providing false, incomplete, or misleading information, or omitting information that would identify a problem in the candidate's background, along with your company's consequences should such false, incomplete, misleading, or omitted information be identified, whether the candidate is still in the hiring process or has already been hired. I talk more on the subject of false information later in the chapter.

Depending on the position being filled, your policies should require additional information from each candidate, such as:

- Resume
- Letters of reference
- Military records
- Copies of diplomas or degrees
- Copies of transcripts

While these may not be required for filling basic-level positions, they are highly recommended when hiring someone at a management level, such as a business manager, office manager, and controller.

I also recommend that somewhere in the application process, whether it is on the application form itself or on a separate form, you seek the candidate's permission to perform a credit check, especially for positions that require access to your company's finances or assets. A credit report cannot be lawfully obtained without the individual's permission, and due to the frequency of identify thefts, individuals will receive notice if inquiries are made into their credit. Therefore, by incorporating candidates' authorization to access their credit report within the application process, you will have their permission and they will receive proper notice if you ultimately access it. I am not suggesting that you obtain a credit report for every candidate for every position you need to fill; I do suggest it be obtained at a minimum for those candidates who become finalists for a position involving access to company finances and assets.

I am also not suggesting that every candidate who has poor credit, who has filed bankruptcy in the past, or who has other negative marks on a credit report should be precluded automatically from your hiring decision. I am simply saying that it is better to know these things exist in a person's background, to allow you to consider them along with all of the candidate's information when making your hiring decision. As discussed earlier, information you receive about a potential employee must be maintained and preserved, and how the information affected your hiring decision could be scrutinized somewhere down the road.

Due Diligence

Once you have candidates complete your application form and provide you with copies of the other documents you require, what should you do next in the hiring process to better protect yourself and your business? The answer is an easy one: due diligence. You need to objectively verify the information they provided to ensure that it is complete and accurate. Candidates often lie or omit details on their applications. According to hiring professionals, during difficult economic times with high unemployment rates, the frequency of lying or embellishing increases as competition for scarce jobs increases.[1] Although providing anything less than complete and accurate information is considered resume fraud, I found through searches on the Internet many terms to describe this growing problem, terms such as embellishing, reaching, exaggerating, tailoring, fudging, shading, and tuning. Reaching, shading, and tuning are all terms that simply mean stretching the truth. I discovered web sites devoted strictly to resume fraud, such as www.fakeresume.com. In some cases the web sites assist potential employers to better screen applicants; other sites are designed to aid candidates in perpetrating these practices.

In what areas can a candidate be less than complete or truthful? Virtually any of the provided information can be false, starting with information relating to a person's identity. In one case I am familiar with, the suspect working in a medical office was terminated from her employment and prosecuted, and her arrest landed her in the local newspapers. An investigative reporter tracked her down while she was pending trial and discovered she was working again, this time in a preschool setting. Further digging by the reporter revealed that the woman had used her maiden name on her application, something the preschool failed to verify. When questioned about why she used her maiden name (as she was still married), she said she had made a mistake on her application. She referred to her error as an oversight. I, however, am sure she didn't use her married name as she had just been in the media for being arrested for stealing from her employer.

In another case, I received a call from a colleague whose client had hired a new finance person. The client told my colleague that the company was aware the man had recently been released from prison but the matter he was sentenced for was a minor theft from his employer. They hired him despite the fact that he had admitted serving time in prison for stealing, and they didn't do any due diligence because he was up-front about what he had done and they considered him rehabilitated. What they failed to identify was that he had served over four years for stealing close to $1.5 million from his employer. Had they dug a bit deeper, they could have learned he had stolen from employers even before the theft he was sentenced for. This man had downplayed what had actually happened, and the client failed to verify his story.

According to a recent 2008 Careerbuilder.com survey, while only 8 percent of respondents admitted to some type of misinformation, 50 percent of hiring managers reported identifying lies on resumes they received.[2] The most common areas of lying and embellishing found through that survey were:

- Job responsibilities: 38 percent
- Skill sets: 18 percent
- Employment start and end dates: 12 percent
- Academic degrees: 10 percent
- Companies/previous employment: 7 percent
- Job titles: 5 percent

Misrepresenting or omitting information on an application or resume is not a new phenomenon, but the frequency of occurrences has likely increased in the past 10 years. A similar survey conducted in 2002 by the American Management Association revealed that 31 percent of resumes contained material misrepresentations about an individual's background.[3]

You need to verify the information provided by candidates applying for any positions.

Personal Information

Start with personal information. Perform a search on the Internet on a candidate's name and address. Using Internet-based resources like Google Earth and Google Satellite, enter the candidate's address to see what actually exists at the address. As simple as it sounds, your search, which will take less than a minute, could be the only means of determining if a house or building actually exists at the address provided. Alternatively, you could drive by the address to see what is there, but searching addresses right from your desk through the Internet will likely be more efficient.

Once you make a hiring decision, the candidate will be required to complete a series of required forms, such as a Form W-4 and a Form I-9. The W-4 will be used to determine the federal taxes to be withheld from the candidate's payroll, and the I-9 will be used to verify that the candidate is in the country legally and eligible for employment. Form I-9 requires you to obtain verification of the candidate's identity and to obtain copies of the verification forms provided. Doing this gives you another opportunity to ensure that the personal information (name, address, date of birth, and Social Security number) match between the application, I-9, verification forms, and any other information provided by the candidate. Take a moment to compare the information before actual employment begins.

Past Employment

As with the candidate's address, perform Internet-based searches of the identified prior employers and their addresses to ensure that they actually exist. I recommend searching the Internet for the business names provided, looking for an address. If I find an address, I search for the address and use the satellite features to see what is located there (i.e., does it look like a commercial building, a house in a residential area, a wooded area, or a big open undeveloped lot?). Candidates do not expect potential employers to drive out and verify that a business actually exists at the address provided, but with these search engines, this verification is relatively easy to perform.

Once you are satisfied that it appears a business does exist at the location provided, contact each past employer to verify employment information supplied. I don't rely on the phone numbers candidates provide. Often if a candidate doesn't want to have a past employer contacted, or worse, wants to ensure that the employer is not contacted due to what he or she could say about the candidate, the contact information provided may be inaccurate or directed toward someone at the company who is not authorized to provide such details but could cover for the candidate.

I rely only on phone numbers publicly listed for the business, found through a search using the Internet, directory assistance, or the old-fashioned phone books. I call the number listed for the business, listen to how the phone is answered, and then ask to be directed to the most appropriate person for my verification. What I am trying to determine is that the information provided is legitimate and reliable, something I will determine by using only phone numbers and information obtained independently of the candidate.

You should want to know as much as possible about the candidate to help you with your hiring decision, but you should expect nothing more than date of hire, date of termination, and whether the individual is eligible for rehiring. As mentioned, most employers have been advised by counsel to provide nothing beyond those items. Once you obtain the dates, compare them with the dates provided by the candidate.

Education

Obtaining copies of diplomas, degrees, and transcripts from candidates is not sufficient to verify that they did in fact earn them by attending the identified schools. Authentic-looking documents can be purchased through web sites for as little as $200, along with corresponding transcripts. For each diploma and degree identified by a candidate, start by verifying that the schools listed actually exist. Once again, Internet-based searches can be performed to help verify their existence.

Once you know that they exist, you need to determine how credible each school is and whether it is accredited. Credential mills do exist, as do correspondence schools whose sole existence is limited to a web site and an 800 number.

Diplomas and degrees can be confirmed with the schools. Based on the position being filled, you should consider verifying that the candidate actually attended, graduated, and was awarded the diploma or degree. It is not uncommon for a candidate to list attendance at a school with no mention of any degree awarded. It is up to you and your verification process to identify when a candidate does this and to ask if he or she graduated and was awarded a degree.

Case Study 1.1   University of Nonexistence

In one of my cases, the controller had stolen funds and was terminated prior to my involvement. When I asked to review the controller's personnel file, I found a copy of his MBA degree along with his MBA transcript—a 4.0 student. Since I had never met the individual, I asked the client if the controller appeared to be a 4.0 MBA graduate. The client's description was consistent with what I expected—someone much less than competent to have performed in that position. I asked the human resources director to contact the school from which he obtained his MBA, and she found the school didn't exist except on paper. There was no known physical address for the school, and a call to the listed 800 number led to an answering system. My question for the client: Why wasn't this information verified prior to hiring the controller?

References

As with all the other information, you should independently verify that the references listed are valid. Search the addresses provided to determine what actually exists at each address. Contact each reference provided, but be aware that it is not uncommon for candidates to list friends and family members as references. Ask each reference how he or she knows the candidate. By asking each reference questions about the candidate, you can learn whether the individual is a legitimate business reference. Ask questions the references would not expect, and listen to their reaction as well as their response. I always like to ask references, since they know the candidate well enough to provide a recommendation, to identify the candidate's greatest strengths and weaknesses.

Ask them for the make and color of the car the candidate drives, or where he or she went to school. (Doing this also helps to corroborate the educational information provided by the candidate.) If the reference cannot answer your non–business-related inquiries about the candidate, you should ask yourself whether the reference is legitimate and how well he or she really knows the candidate.

Criminal and Civil History Checks

Depending on the position you are filling, you should consider running a criminal background check on the final candidates. However, don't be complacent with results that turn up nothing. Here is a word of caution regarding the results of these searches: Individuals could have a criminal history and not appear on the search results for at least three reasons.

1. The individual may have committed the crimes as a juvenile. In that case, records prior to turning 18 years old would not be available for disclosure.

11

2. The individual could have been involved in criminal activity in the past, but for a number of reasons, the crime might not have been prosecuted and/or the charges might have been subsequently dropped. The criminal history will reveal criminal convictions only, if anything at all.

3. The individual could have received a special sentence, such as accelerated rehabilitation available for first-time offenders. His or her criminal record would be erased as part of that program after three years with no further criminal activity and therefore would not be reported in the search results.

A good resource to search for prior criminal activity is in newspapers around the country. By using a commercial database service, such as LexisNexis, or simply searching online through Google News, you may locate an article involving the individual in a local news story. Here, too, it is important not to place sole reliance on the fact that nothing was found, particularly in the case of embezzlements, because statistically, only one in nine cases ever appears in the public eye.

You should be able to access an individual's civil history relatively easily. You can access most states' judicial system records via web sites. Once you find the judicial site, you can search the person's history based on last and first names. In my home state of Connecticut, the web site is at www.jud.state.ct.us/jud2.htm. Select the venue (civil, family, motor vehicles, small claims) and enter the individual's name into the fields provided to conduct your search.

The mere fact that an individual has a prior criminal and/or civil history doesn't necessarily make him or her a bad person or a poor choice for employment. However, if you are seriously considering the candidate for a position, consider discussing his or her past to ensure that you have all the information to make an informed decision. Also, review the candidate's history in light of the job responsibilities he or she will have once hired. Although an individual may be ideal for a position, a history of stealing from employers may make the person less than desirable in a position that gives him or her access to your company's finances or other assets.

As mentioned earlier, be prudent about how you use the results of these searches in your hiring decisions. You should discuss this issue with counsel to ensure that a candidate doesn't make some type of complaint or take action against you because you excluded him or her from consideration due to information you discovered.

Credit Checks

Another important consideration in your hiring process is whether you run a credit report on the finalists being considered for a position. Here, too, you should proceed with advice of counsel, as many laws protect an individual's personal credit and identity information. The most important thing to remember, as mentioned earlier, is that you *cannot* run a person's credit report without his or her permission, and in response to new laws, the individual will receive notice if his or her credit is run. Therefore, as part of your hiring process, you need to obtain candidates' permission to run their credit report. I believe all applicants should provide permission to access their credit history on every job application. It may not make sense and would be costly to obtain every applicant's credit history, but you can identify and screen out candidates who are not willing to have their credit history obtained early in the process.

As with the criminal and civil histories, the mere fact that an individual has less-than-stellar credit history does not in and of itself make him or her a bad person or poor hire. However, it would be better to know during the screening process if a candidate has poor credit and a history of bankruptcies, especially if the successful hire will have access to your business's finances. It goes without saying that you need to be prudent in how you use the credit information you obtain. You should discuss this issue with counsel as well to avoid unwanted legal issues.

Hiring Time

Once you have narrowed down the candidates, verified their information, and made your hiring decision, you need to continue thinking about protecting your business. Consider establishing a policy outlining confidentiality and information proprietary to your business, such as customer lists, sales and product information, and trade secrets. The policy should indicate that all information provided within employment at the business is the property of the business. Upon termination of employment, all property of the company is to be immediately returned to the business, including any electronic records.

Theft of company information happens all the time. Your confidentiality and proprietary information policies should also state that your company has a zero tolerance policy. Any instances of theft or fraud of any company assets, finances, or information will be subject to disciplinary action up to and including termination of employment, and the individual will be held criminally and/or civilly responsible if it is shown that his or her actions caused any harm or damage to the business. During their orientation, all new employees should be provided with a copy of the policy and be required to sign it. The signed forms should be maintained in their personnel files to provide proof that they were made aware of the policies.

Such policies establish the strict ethical tone of your company at the inception of a new employee's employment and should also act as a deterrent. Consider having your attorney draft such policies for your use and distribution to all existing employees and every new hire.

Case Study 1.2   "My" Clients Go Wherever I Go

An accountant left his position with a large accounting firm after many years of employment, having reached the level of senior manager. As part of his employment, the accountant had signed a written agreement that the client lists and staff belonged to the firm. The accountant was prohibited from poaching clients or staff of the firm for a two-year period after terminating employment. Within weeks of starting with a smaller firm, the accountant began contacting clients he had serviced through his old firm. In addition, the new firm sent out a mailing specifically targeting clients of the former firm.

When partners of the former firm learned of the poaching activity, they contacted counsel, and a cease order was drafted and sent out to the accountant. The partners then initiated an investigation into the accountant's activities during the last few months of his employment. By searching the server backups, e-mail activity, and user tracking logs, the firm was able to determine that the individual had copied the files pertaining to his clients in the weeks leading up to his resignation. Further, they found e-mail communications between the accountant and individuals at his new firm regarding business "development" opportunities (i.e., bringing clients over to the new firm). The firm also determined that the accountant had run reports regarding clients of the firm other than those whom he had serviced.

(continued)

(Continued)

The partners, through counsel, demanded the return of client and firm information and threatened professional, civil, and criminal actions if the poaching did not stop immediately and if the proprietary information was not returned. The accountant never expected this response from the former firm, nor did his new firm. Without admitting to any wrongdoing, the new firm agreed to cease all "marketing" activity toward clients of the former firm. As far as the return of any information, the new firm and accountant indicated they had no information to return. (Here they were likely well advised by counsel, as anything else would have proven that the accountant had in fact stolen the data.) The former firm monitored the situation for months, but nothing further ever happened with any of its clients.

■ ■ ■

Now that you have made your hiring decision, the process of learning as much as possible about potential employees shifts to the process of knowing and monitoring your existing employees, the focus of discussions in Chapter 2.

Notes

1. Kathy Gurchiek, "Mensa Membership, Kennedy Kinship among Outrageous Resume Lies," Society for Human Resource Management, August 14, 2008; available at: www.shrm.org/Publications/HRNews/Pages/OutrageousResumeLies.aspx.
2. "Nearly Half of Employers Have Caught a Lie on a Resume," July 30, 2008; available at: www.careerbuilder.com/share/aboutus/pressreleasesdetail.aspx?id=pr448&sd=7/30/2008&ed=7/30/2099.
3. Scott Moritz, "Don't Get Burned by Smiling CEO Candidates," *Fraud Magazine* (September/October 2002). Available online at: www.acfe.com/resources/view.asp?ArticleID=198.

Hiring the Right Employees: Considerations

Application Process	**Completed**
Candidates complete written job application.	❑
Candidates provide resume and any other required information.	❑
Applications include permission to obtain credit information.	❑
Applications are screened for applicability to position being filled.	❑
Potential hires are identified.	❑

Due Diligence	
Past employers are verified for existence.	❑
Past employers are contacted.	❑
Education is verified.	❑
References are validated.	❑
References are contacted.	❑
Criminal history search is considered and obtained if warranted.	❑
Civil history search is considered and obtained if warranted.	❑
Credit history is considered and obtained if warranted.	❑
Screening process is completed.	❑

Hiring	
Offer extended to candidate.	❑
Company policies provided to new hire upon commencement of employment.	❑

(continued)

(Continued)

Signed acknowledgments placed in employee's ❏
personnel file, along with the application and
other information they provided or you
obtained during the hiring process.

CHAPTER 2

Know Your Employees

As a fraud investigator, I interact with the victims of the crimes as well as the perpetrators. These crimes go beyond the mere theft of company assets, funds, and information, and include a violation of trust established between the employer and the responsible employee. Friendships are often formed over time between small business owners and their employees, often very close relationships and bonds, and it is not uncommon for business owners to describe their offices as family-like environments. Many owners take a personal interest in the lives and issues of their employees, and vice versa, especially employees with longevity and who have been loyal, trustworthy, and accommodating to the needs of the owner and the business.

When a trusted, long-term employee is found to have been stealing from the company, the owner and the coworkers take it very personally, especially in the small business setting. Unfortunately, it is almost always the employee who is most trustworthy, who is like family, and who has been there the longest who is found to have stolen funds and/or assets. Having seen it time and again in my cases, the emotional toll these cases have on the owners and employees often surpasses the financial impact.

In my experience, these cases follow a path similar to the grieving process, also known as the five stages of grief.[1] The first stage is denial. "You're wrong!" "It can't be that, there must be another explanation." "That person would never do that." "I have spent the last *(you name how many years)* with this person, side by side; it can't be them." The victim is in utter disbelief that someone so close would do such a thing.

Next comes the second stage—anger. In my experience, both the owner and the employees become angry, and this is when you get the real dirt on what the person has been doing, in the business and in his or her personal life. Employers and employees alike feel such a sense of violation, they want revenge: "Lock him up!" "Put her in jail!" Recognizing when a victim and the staff enter this stage and managing their anger can be an important challenge, especially if large sums are involved and the owner has made personal or financial sacrifices (even position cuts and decreases in wages) due to the poor financial conditions, only to learn it was all the result of a dishonest employee.

With time, the owner and employees will move to the third stage—bargaining. Not always, but often, the victim wants to find a way to resolve the matter. Fraud investigations take time, three to six months at a minimum, and can last for years. The longer the matter is unresolved, the longer the daily reminder remains in victims' lives. Bargaining could involve the owner trying to settle the matter, simply to seek closure. Unfortunately, most fraud cases drag out too long, often due to the actions or inactions of the suspect and/or his or her attorney. Delay, delay, delay seems to be the tactic of choice, until eventually parties just want closure and at any cost (typically at a minimal cost and consequence). The longer a matter remains open and unresolved, the more depressed the victim and coworkers can become. They seek justice and a consequence but see slow progress, if any, toward that end. Depression is the fourth stage.

The final stage is acceptance. Owners who talk to enough fellow business owners and colleagues are likely to find they are not alone in being victimized. Employee fraud is common, perhaps more so today than in the past, and many victims never recover any funds, receive an apology, or obtain the justice desired. It seems to be a pattern in these cases. The old adage "misery loves company" applies: If you can introduce the victim to others with similar stories, even without closure the victim can find a way to move on.

The perpetrators of employee fraud follow a similar process through the five stages of grief once they are caught. First comes denial, followed closely by anger. I saw this firsthand in a case that we controlled but could have gone terribly wrong (Case Study 2.1).

Case Study 2.1　Expect the Unexpected

A store manager was being investigated by us for skimming sales from the store. Before the manager knew of our involvement, we reviewed trends and financial reports for the store and compared them to the same information for other similar stores. It was clear there was something happening in the trends within the manager's store. Based on the personal lives and issues of each of the five employees who worked in the store in conjunction with who had access to financial transactions, we believed the manager was the likely target of an investigation, at least initially. When we first visited the store, we planned to interview all five employees on that day, ending with the manager. The plan worked, and we interviewed the manager last. After an hour it was clear she was hiding something, and once her bottom lip started quivering, we knew there was a story to be told. We convinced her to tell us what had been happening at the store, and through the tears, she confessed to

(continued)

(Continued)

stealing the receipts. She was placed on paid administrative leave, told not to return until she received a call from human resources, and walked out of the store.

We continued our investigation and determined that she did in fact divert deposits from the store and that no other employees could have committed the thefts. We quantified the thefts and prepared an insurance claim. As part of the resolution, the manager was called in and asked to resign or be terminated (a common approach to ending these matters). She showed up at the scheduled time, pled her case, and reviewed the options presented to her. She was advised to take time to make her decision and to seek counsel if needed to help her. She signed a resignation and release and, through tears again, apologized for her actions. As she left the building, her tears turned to anger. She was very upset, screaming and yelling, ranting and raving. Eventually she left, very angry. Thankfully she did not return with a weapon seeking retaliation or revenge (as we have seen all too frequently in recent history). Prudently we did contact the police and apprised them of the situation, and perhaps their presence deterred her from returning. In any event, what could have been a very bad situation ended on a good note. Never let your guard down, not even for basic financial crimes.

After anger comes bargaining: Can we work this out? If more of the perpetrators in my past had come to this stage sooner and actually worked things out, they likely would have avoided criminal prosecution and perhaps even jail. However, some individuals just can't take responsibility for their actions, and deny their way to prison. I experienced this with one of my students during a course I teach on forensic accounting. I caught him using another student's paper from a previous semester. When I called him on it, he denied, denied, and denied. Then he became angry and counterattacked with allegations against me. Just like the embezzlers I investigate, I told him it was going to get ugly for him unless we worked it out. Since I caught him plagiarizing, the consequences at my disposal included expulsion from the program and the school—a heavy consequence as he was in his last semester before receiving his degree. Next came the bargaining: How can we work this out? The problem was that I had already elevated the issue due to his personal attacks on my credibility, and now he needed to bargain with my supervisor at the school, the director of the program. Needless to say, he lost. He elected to be removed from my class and was prevented from graduating that semester but was allowed to take another course during the next session to graduate at a later date. I thought the director gave him a huge break—he could have lost everything. Imagine a student defrauding a fraud class—go figure.

Moving past bargaining, the suspect commonly enters the period of depression. It is not uncommon for fraud suspects to attempt suicide and in some cases be successful at it. This is never the desired outcome; I get depressed when I learn of such grave decisions made by a suspect.

The last stage is acceptance. Those suspects who know they will be going to prison, with no way of avoiding it, eventually prepare to go away for their time. They have outrun the consequence as long as possible, but the time has come to accept responsibility for their actions. Not everyone ends up in prison. Actually, too few financial criminals end up serving any time. More often they are forced to pay fines, make restitution (to the extent they can), and serve some alternative sentence, like probation, house arrest, and community service. Regardless, at some point they have to accept that they did in fact do the deeds of which they are accused. They got caught, and now they have to face the fact that "it is what it is."

Why Is Knowing Your Employees Important?

Employees for the most part do not obtain employment with your company for the sole intention of stealing assets, funds, and information from your business. Despite what one former convicted fraudster recently said in an interview, where he recommended abandoning Ronald Reagan's "Trust but verify" approach and suggested replacing it with his "Trust no one, and verify everything," I believe there are decent, honest, and trustworthy individuals within our society. I choose to believe more people are honest than dishonest, at least when it comes to handling their employers' finances. Unlike the convicted felon's warped vision of society where everyone is much like himself, an untrustworthy financial criminal, employees in general are not as corrupt as he would want us to believe.

Here's what typically happens in employee embezzlement cases. An employee experiences a change in personal life, encounters an insurmountable financial crisis, or suffers from a personal addiction of some type (drinking, drugs, gambling, etc.). The change could be a health issue, higher education need, death, divorce, loss of spouse's income, imminent bankruptcy, or avoidance of foreclosure, and the impact is subjective to each individual. No two individuals would handle the crisis the same way. Unfortunately, the employee looks toward opportunities within his or her employment to satisfy the issue, albeit temporarily, and rationalizes the thought process in support of his or her actions. Once all three elements of the "fraud triangle" (opportunity, financial need, and rationalization) have been met by the individual, the employee "borrows" funds. The rationalization may include an intention to repay the funds, but if the borrowing simply ended with repayment, there would not be a loss to the employer. That's how these matters begin.

The rationalization and initial theft becomes a bigger problem when the employee fails to put the funds back and then does it all over again, and again, and again, intending to put it all back but moving rapidly away from the ability to repay the funds. What often starts out as a snowball at the top of the hill quickly accelerates down the slippery slope, growing in size and frequency as it builds and builds, until it becomes a huge snow boulder rolling out of control. These cases start with taking as little as $20 or $100 and end in the discovery of tens and hundreds of thousands of dollars missing. The victims are often overwhelmed by how long the employee has been stealing and how much has accumulated due to the thefts.

As a small business owner, you have to recognize when things are going on in the personal lives of your employees. Events or crises could create an insurmountable financial need. You need to pay attention to the opportunity available for those individuals, and watch things more closely to ensure that those areas do not get exploited.

Open Communications

By establishing a protocol and work climate that encourages discussing issues with all employees, you may be able to thwart misguided visions of using company funds to solve personal financial issues. At a minimum you will have a better understanding of what is happening in employees' personal lives that not only creates a potential for fraud against you but also decreases their productivity and lowers their morale. Employees would also know you were aware of their situations, which could act as a deterrent to their eyeing your business as their personal checkbook.

You need to develop and communicate a means for employees to discuss personal matters with you, and you also need to create a means for employees to bring to your attention information and concerns about fellow employees. In many of my investigations, I learned that fellow employees knew, or at least suspected, that something was happening within the business. All too often the suspected person was a supervisor, and employees had no means to bring the information to the attention of the owner.

Employees need to know that they have a duty to report suspected unauthorized or fraudulent acts by other employees, including their supervisors, but they also need to know how to do so.

What Should You Watch for in Your Employees?

Employees who are dishonest and are committing some type of fraud or unauthorized activity tend to behave in unusual ways. However, not all unusual behavior is an indication of fraud. The key is to know your employees and watch for changes in their behavior. People who are unwilling to take vacation time, or who take a vacation only if no one does their job while they are away, are people you should pay attention to in order to determine why other employees can't do their job while they are away. Are they being protective of their position, or are they hiding something? Employees tend to become defensive, building a barrier between themselves and everyone else, to keep prying eyes out of areas they control.

Listen to the discussions within your business, which is not to say that you should eavesdrop on private conversations. Know where your employees live and, if they are married, what their spouses do. Know their family life and where their kids go to school. See the cars they and their spouses drive. Observe how they dress, the jewelry they wear, and where they shop.

Listen to what they do on their personal time. Likely there are clues in these areas to alert you that there could be potential issues in your business. Living beyond their means is a common reason why employees divert funds for personal use. Entitlement and desperation have been the primary motivators I have seen in these cases in the past several years, along with a few true financial needs or addictions, such as gambling debts, foreclosures, and educational costs for family members.

I contend that you will know someone in your business is stealing funds long before evidence surfaces revealing their scheme. In addition to behavior, watch for other indications that someone could be stealing assets, funds, or information. Here is a list of things I recommend you watch for in your business:

- Unusual employee behavior
- Noticeable personality changes in an employee
- Employee living beyond his or her means
- Employee never takes any time off
- Undeposited customer payments/cash receipts
- Customer accounts receivable growing larger and older
- Unexplained drop in cash flows (especially with increases in sales and volume)
- Unexplained rise in unpaid vendors
- Missing documents or sloppy record keeping
- Accounts out of balance or unreconciled
- Unexplained differences in reconciliations of balances
- Unauthorized access to computer files

■ ■ ■

Beyond knowing your employees, you need to ensure that you have implemented adequate internal controls and procedures to safeguard your assets, funds, and information.

Cash receipts coming into your business fuel the cash flows for everything else, and are the logical place to begin an assessment of controls and procedures.

Note

1. *The Stages of Grief*, available at: www.memorialhospital.org/library/general/stress-THE-3.html.

Know Your Employees: Considerations

	Completed
In General	
Get to know your employees.	❏

Communications

Consider establishing and communicating to employees a means to discuss personal financial issues with you.	❏
Communicate to employees their fiduciary responsibilities as employees, including their duty to report suspected activity to you.	❏
Establish and explain to employees a means for them to communicate information regarding suspected activity of fellow employees.	❏

Vigilance

Know and monitor your employees.	❏
Watch for unusual employee behavior or changes in employee personality, attitude, or behavior.	❏
Monitor employees' lifestyles and watch for any noticeable changes or activity inconsistent with their lifestyle.	❏
Monitor for other common signs of a potential problem.	❏
Ensure employees take vacations and time off and that someone else is doing their job while they are away.	❏

(continued)

29

(Continued)

Consider rearranging job responsibilities, ❏
create cross-training opportunities, and
have employees cover other employees'
areas of responsibilities on a regular basis.

Responses to Potential Signs or Indications

If any signs become apparent, determine the ❏
employee's areas of responsibility, and
opportunities.

Increase your level of scrutiny in the areas ❏
identified, looking for any signs that an
area of opportunity has been exploited.

Consider implementing additional controls or ❏
reassigning/rearranging responsibilities,
even temporarily, to address your
concerns.

Consider consulting with your outside ❏
accountant or someone experienced in
these matters to quietly look further into
the employee's responsibilities and areas
of opportunities, to see if anything has
occurred.

CHAPTER 3

Sales, Cash Receipts, and Collections

Here's Where Everything Starts

Arguably the most important accounting cycle in every business, making sales and collecting payments is the starting point for all the other financial processes and likely is the reason for every business to exist. Successful execution of sales and collections provides the cash flows to the company, and without either one, there would be no need for payables, cash disbursements, payroll, and all the other accounting cycles, as there would be no cash available to fund those areas. The revenue cycle is where I have always started my evaluations of businesses from both the operational and financial perspectives. If there were no sales, or if there were no collections on sales made on account, there would be little to no need for any internal controls, policies, and procedures, as there would be no business.

Beyond being the most important aspect of securing the financial health of the company, the cash receipts cycle has been exploited time and again by dishonest employees diverting coveted sales and collections away from the company for personal gain. Over the past several years, it is my opinion that thefts within the revenue cycle have become the method of choice for untrustworthy employees, and it is where I have spent the largest amount of time. Even if your business doesn't process much in the way of transactions in the form of cash, the schemes perpetrated within the revenue cycle extend beyond the diversion of cash. Therefore, your focus needs to be directed toward all the different ways in which your business gets paid for sales or services.

Recording and Tracking Sales

A logical starting point is the recording of sales. Depending on the nature of your business, sales recording could be accomplished through the use of a cash register at a customer counter within a small retail location or could be through a formal invoicing system. Sales can be as simple as a local dairy recording cash-only sales of milk, eggs, ice cream, and other farm-produced products at the single-location dairy store, or can be as complicated as a multilocation distributor of auto parts located throughout the United States. Clearly the nature of the sale items or services provided, along with the size of the company's operations, will have a direct impact on the level of sophistication found within the systems implemented over recording and tracking sales. One would expect a fairly simple stand-alone register system for smaller entities and a fully networked sales system integrated with ordering, invoicing, and receivables modules for the largest of businesses. The context or industry of each business would also be a factor. The system I would expect to find tracking sales within a restaurant would be different from the one used within a large retailer like The Home Depot and would be different again from the one utilized by a local sand and gravel supplier.

The main point is that every business needs to have a system to track and record sales to ensure that all sales have been captured, tracked, and recorded. The sales and collection process may start and end simultaneously, such as with retail sales where payment is collected at the time of delivery of goods, food, or service, or they may occur at two distinctly different times, such as when a business invoices for sales and services and subsequently collects customer payments based on their payment terms.

Only a book dedicated solely to the revenue cycle could attempt a complete discussion of appropriate sales and collection policies and procedures for every possible context. That is not the intention of this book. Books and information are readily available to address specific industries and business contexts. The goal of this book is to discuss several of the common vulnerabilities within most businesses.

Retail Sales

Employee thefts within the sales process for retailers can be one of the hardest issues to address from a prevention perspective. There are many ways dishonest employees can skim sales and divert payments away from the business, and even with the best-designed and best-implemented procedures, employees often seem to find ways to steal sales proceeds. One of the hardest areas to control is with cash sales, such as within a coffee shop, ice cream parlor, or bar/lounge. High-volume, low-dollar sales transactions will always be one of the most vulnerable areas for owners. Determining how many drinks were poured, or how many scoops were served, is difficult to control, and often the cost of controls outweighs any potential benefits. That's not to say that business owners should ignore controls to prevent employee thefts, but emphasis must be placed on detecting possible thefts as early as possible where preventive controls failed. As part of the detection approach, business owners should consider video surveillance of employees within the sales areas to both monitor for dishonest behavior and act as a deterrent.

Creating expectations with customers would be a good starting point. A regional chain of pharmacies in my area have a sign posted at each checkout register that states, "$5.00 off your next visit if we fail to issue you a register receipt." A chain of ice cream stores has similar signs posted in all of its stores. Why do you think the owners of these chains want to give a customer a coupon for $5.00 off their next visit? The answer is easy: The owner wants the sign to create customer expectations regarding a register receipt. If customers are told to expect a receipt, they will be watching for one. In the event they don't receive one, one hopes they will ask for it and also receive their coupon. The coupons should be prenumbered to track who issued them to customers as well as who redeemed them. The goal of this policy is to better ensure that every sale gets run through the store's register or sales system, which makes it much more difficult for a dishonest employee to skim sales from the store. Employees who are found to have issued too many $5.00 coupons should be terminated. It is likely that they tried to skim sales by not ringing sales through the register and were caught by customers too many times, or they simply didn't comply with store policies and procedures by providing customers with their register receipt. Either way, they need to go.

Whether using registers or point-of-sale terminals, a designated individual should be assigned to each checkout area, and policies should prohibit the sharing of registers or terminals where practical. The most frequent context I have seen businesses implementing these measures is in grocery stores. Cashiers are assigned their own drawers and are responsible for their drawers and corresponding sales for the entire shift. At random times during the shift the supervisor will move a cashier to another line, causing him or her to close out the terminal, close out the drawer, and go to another line, where the cashier needs to sign in and start over. In some cases the drawer follows the cashier; in other instances the drawer is taken and reconciled, and the cashier starts the new line with a new drawer. A combination of both practices with no identifiable pattern may prove to be the most effective. Cashiers would never know when they could be moved, closed out, and reconciled.

Consider creating a policy requiring all checkout areas to remain clear of any clutter or items. It is common for dishonest employees to track how much they skimmed during their shift, from the obvious writing down amounts in a notebook to using inconspicuous items representing their tracking. One scheme could involve using coins, each representing the dollar amount skimmed, such as a dime representing $10 and a nickel, $5. Another could involve large and small paper clips, the large one representing $20 or $10 and the smaller one, $5 or $1. Virtually any objects can be used, limited only to the creativity of the individual. These objects are used to track the skim so that the employees can balance their drawers. If all clutter is removed around the checkout area, including calculators commonly used to calculate the total sale, sales tax, and change without using the register, there should be no way to track the skim, leaving individuals to rely on their memory. Look around the checkout areas the next time you are in a store and see what you notice around the register.

Employees who ring sales should not be authorized to process voids or returns. A designated individual should be required to approve all voids and returns, either through a separate key to the register or a separate user ID or password on a point-of-sale system. Cashiers should not have access to either controls. Alternatively, if capacity is an issue within the smallest businesses, employees could be authorized to process voids or returns up to a certain dollar amount before requiring approval from an owner or designated individual. In either case, there should also be monitoring of the daily activity of employees responsible for retail sales, along with analysis of the transactions, including trending and a comparison of the activity between different employees. One individual identified with more frequent voids compared to the other employees, or with frequent voids just below the threshold requiring supervisor approval, could alert you to a potential skim.

Case Study 3.1   Retailer "Voids" Worker's Employment for Misuse of Voids

I was speaking at a seminar about preventing employee embezzlement and implementing internal controls. At the end of the session an attendee came up and asked to speak with me. He indicated that he was the manager of a local grocery store chain and that recently the store had identified an unusual trend in one cashier's activity. He said the cashier was a local high school student whose family the store knew very well, as they were longtime customers. He said the cashier was an honor student and was very active and popular in high school, and seemed to be an ideal employee for the position. The activity showed that she had more $1.99 voided items on her reports than any other cashier, and on some days there could be many, many voids, one right after another. He said they tried monitoring her covertly, but nothing apparent was noticed in watching her ring up customers. He said the store didn't want to offend her or the family by confronting her yet, especially if a plausible explanation could be found without her ever knowing she was under scrutiny. He asked me what I thought was happening and how the store should handle the issue.

I asked him if the stores had a policy on voided transactions, such as a dollar threshold that allowed cashiers to process below the amount and required a cashier supervisor

---

to process for higher amounts. He said the store policy was set at $2.00 per voided transaction. I asked him if they ever noticed any patterns of voids for any other amount other than $1.99, coincidently just below the $2.00 limit. He said there were no void amounts other than $1.99. I told him that the activity was simply bizarre. How could a cashier have no voided transactions for any amount other than $1.99? I said that information told me the cashier was a careful cashier in ringing through sales, as less attentive cashiers often result in requiring voids, but for varying amounts. I told him that based on the limited information he provided, it appeared the cashier was skimming the register in increments of $1.99. I figured it could be one of two things.

1. The cashier could be processing a consistent item she controlled as a void to withdraw the funds from her drawer. Reviewing her checkout area while she worked could identify what she was using to process the void (i.e., what she was scanning as a voided or returned item).
2. She could be processing voids during sales to her friends and family, which could be why she was so popular.

I suggested they continue monitoring her activity and watch to see who goes through her line, and compare what is observed to her activity reports to find any patterns. Either way, if the store continued to monitor her activity, the manager should be able to identify what she was doing with the voids.

He thanked me for the advice and for listening, and I never heard from him again. However, I have been to the store on many occasions, and since the majority of their cashiers are high school females, I never knew if the cashier they suspected was one of the individuals who had rung up my sales.

Your procedures should consider making each employee responsible for counting and reconciling his or her own drawer and activity at the end of each shift. Have employees complete their balancing with someone else present, and investigate any differences before employees leave. Have employees sign their reports or register tapes, and if a form is used to reconcile the activity, have the employees sign their form. Enact a policy that if their drawer is off more than a set dollar amount on more than one occasion, the second time it occurs results in a warning and the third time the individual is terminated.

As mentioned earlier, consider installing surveillance systems to monitor any areas where sales and collections could occur. One company installed a surveillance system that was integrated into its sales system. System parameters were established, and every time any cashier processed a void for more than $1.99, the system took a picture of the employee at the terminal as well as the customer, and e-mailed the image to the owner. This allowed the owner to know every time a void greater than $1.99 was processed each day as well as identified the employee and customer actually involved each time, allowing the owner to determine if a pattern existed.

Another detection measure could be the use of mystery shoppers to visit your business locations. Mystery shopping services send individuals into the business posing as customers. The timing of their visits and the identity of the individuals are unknown to the employees (and often the owners). To be most effective, mystery shoppers should be told prior to their visit of the owner's expectations of the location as well as the policies and procedures employees should be following. The mystery shoppers would then shop your business, interact with employees, and observe the location as well as the activity, all without the knowledge of your employees. Mystery shoppers then report their experience to the owner.

You need to remain vigilant and monitor sales activity closely to ensure that all sales are processed through the system and to ensure that all sale proceeds are properly deposited into the business account.

Credit Sales

By way of differentiating credit sales from retail sales just discussed, credit sales would include any sale of products, whether purchased inventory or manufactured items, to customers on account (recorded through accounts receivable) with a future payment expected from a customer for each sale (also known as sales on account). Regardless of the product sold, the ordered items are delivered to the customer based on preauthorized terms and hopefully within a short time after delivery the customer remits payment. Payments are often received in the form of a check payable to the business, but they could also be received electronically into the business bank account.

You should have policies and procedures to control the acceptance of any new customers as well as the extension of credit terms to any customers. Ideally an owner or designated individual should be responsible for accepting new customers and assigning initial credit limits. System controls should prevent unauthorized employees from entering new customers or making changes to existing customers. One scheme involves a dishonest employee adding a fictitious customer to the sales system and extending generous credit terms to him or her. A variation is to make changes to an existing customer involved in the scheme. The employee then processes sales orders to the fictitious customer in the hopes that the product will be shipped to an address controlled by the employee, such as a vacant warehouse. Once sufficient product has shipped, maximizing the fictitious customer's credit limit, the employee leaves the company. Subsequent collection efforts for payment on the shipments prove fruitless, as the product is gone without a trace from the warehouse, and the demographic information for the fictitious customer is found to be invalid.

Where practical, individuals responsible for shipping product should be independent and separate from individuals responsible for recording sales and processing invoices to customers. A procedure should be implemented to match shipping information with customer invoicing on a regular basis to ensure that every shipment to a customer is supported by a sales invoice posted within the system.

Your goal in implementing controls and procedures over credit sales is to ensure that every sale made on account is properly recorded and reflected within the sales and accounts receivable systems, allowing subsequent procedures to rely on those systems to collect all payments due your business.

Services

Similar to the previous discussion of ensuring that all sales are properly recorded and invoiced within the system, all services rendered by your business need to be reconciled on a regular basis to customer invoices. Depending on the nature of services provided, the "sales" process may end at the time the service is completed, generally on the same day, or it could extend for days, weeks, and even months. For example, in the case of medical and dental practices, every patient encounter should be reconciled to a corresponding charge (sale) posted into the practice's billing system on a daily basis. The patient came in, was seen and treated, and the sales process ended when the patient was checked out. A similar expectation would exist for a company that services residential furnaces. A repairperson is sent out on scheduled appointments and at the end of each day should return with the company vehicle along with completed paperwork for each service call completed. There should be an invoice posted into the system for each customer serviced on a daily basis, and a procedure should exist to match work schedules to customer invoices.

Conversely, an electrician or plumber may work several days or weeks on a project. Invoicing could be completed at set intervals based on achieving completion points or could be completed once all work has been performed. A contract should typically exist for projects that extend over a period, and the invoices posted to the system should be compared to the contracts to ensure that all billing has been captured and completed.

On an even larger scale would be projects that extend over much longer periods of time. These projects should be memorialized within formal purchase orders and contracts, with the invoicing and payment terms identified. Invoicing likely occurs on a percentage-of-completion basis, such as with construction contractors and tradespeople. You should have procedures in place to monitor the contracts and invoices on a regular basis to ensure that all invoicing opportunities have been completed and that all invoices have been properly reflected within the systems.

As with sales, your goal of implementing controls and procedures over service invoices is to ensure that every completed service performed is properly recorded, invoiced, and reflected within the sales and accounts receivable systems, allowing subsequent procedures to rely on those systems to collect all payments due to your business.

A risk exists with any business that provides services where employees could complete calls, appointments, or even entire projects outside the company without the knowledge or permission of the owner. Such work that appropriately should be completed through the business could be completed "on the side," at night or on the weekends, and is often completed at a discount if the customer pays the individual directly in cash.

The employee diverts billable business away from your company and keeps the payments for personal use, depriving you of those funds. It is also common for employees to use your tools and equipment and to purchase the parts and materials for these side jobs through the company, avoiding any costs on these jobs and maximizing personal profits. Tools and equipment should be secured and not made available to employees when not in use for company business. Parts and materials purchased should be assigned to specific jobs, and procedures should be in place to ensure that customer invoices exist for all customers identified within the purchases. You should also consider installing global positioning system (GPS) devices in every company vehicle and monitoring vehicle usage to ensure that employees are not using company vehicles for personal purposes. Systems are available to track and report all the activity of each vehicle, from times they are at each location through speeds and idling times.

Case Study 3.2   Under the Table

Two summers ago the water heater failed in our basement, resulting in a mess of rusty water. Our water heater is of the type that is attached to our oil furnace. A furnace crew came out as well as a water heater crew, both from the same oil company we use. Within a short time the old water heater was removed from our basement, the mess was cleaned (although the stains on the floor are permanent), and the new water heater was installed. At one point during the day, I was speaking with the water heater guy, a very large, hefty man who carried the water heater in from his truck (a really big guy). We somehow got into a conversation about income and taxes, and he said to me (someone he had never previously met) that he did furnace and water heater work on the side on weekends, always for a discount and always in cash. He said cash was king and that doing the jobs allowed him to make more money and keep the income off his tax returns. He then told me that if we ever had any issues with the water heater or our furnace (which someday would need to be replaced), I should just call him directly, and I could "save a bunch of money" by having him do the work for cash. He said he would be doing the work anyway if I called the oil company and had the work completed. I know so many people who have done that, only to run into problems down the line with workmanship or warranty issues. The savings in cash today will not outweigh the headaches down the road when the oil company has no record of doing the work and won't service the system. Ignoring the obvious case of tax fraud, this guy is stealing customer sales from his employer and therefore stealing revenue and profits from the business.

A similar issue happened with the two men who installed our carpeting in our computer/family room. We bought carpeting from a local retailer and arranged to have it installed. The store clearly utilizes subcontractors to do its installations. The store charges for the installation and pays the contractors once the job is complete. So one would think the contractors would be loyal to the stores that refer work to them. As the men finished installing the carpet, they asked where we bought it. We told them the name of the local store. The man took out a business card and wrote down his phone number on it. He told us that he had access to all the same flooring at a significantly reduced price and that in the future if we needed any flooring we should call him directly to save a bunch of money. How is that not stealing business away from the local flooring company?

Another variation of this scheme is for the employee to divert projects to competing businesses, only to receive a kickback from the competing business owner. Although it may be difficult to prevent a dishonest employee from diverting business away from the company, closely tracking the activity of your employees along with following up on any lost projects and bids could help identify a potential problem.

Collections

Most businesses that invoice customers for sales or services receive physical checks from customers for payment. Payments can be received directly at the company through the mail or through a post office box controlled by the company. Some businesses also allow customers to bring their payments in person to the company, especially those customers with a past credit history. Larger customers often remit their payments electronically into the company's bank account, while others can mail their payments directly to a bank-sponsored lockbox established for the benefit of the business.

One way or another, payments are received by every business and need to be tracked, recorded, deposited, and reconciled on a regular basis. The goal of implementing controls, policies, and procedures over cash receipts is to ensure that every payment due the business is timely and properly received, recorded, and deposited into the company's bank account.

Based on my experience, the diversion of customer payments has become the number-one scheme of choice for dishonest employees. Regardless of who the check is made payable to (typically payable to the business), individuals divert these payments and conceal their diversion within the accounts receivable system. The diverted checks are then converted to cash; the prevailing method seems to be by depositing the diverted checks directly into the perpetrator's personal bank account via automated teller machines (ATMs). To conceal their diversion, payments, debit memos, or other adjustments are posted to the customer's account balance, removing the diverted balance from the company's accounts receivable system.

Therefore, preventive and detection controls need to be implemented in the areas of payment processing, payment posting, debit memo and adjustment posting, and ongoing monitoring of the company's accounts receivable details.

The key to assessing the risk of employee theft and embezzlement lies within the employees' opportunities to steal funds from your company. If employees do not have access to the funds, it only makes sense that they cannot divert the funds, as is the case with the use of a bank-controlled lockbox arrangement. A company contracts with a bank to control a post office box for the benefit of the business. All customer payments are directed to the post office box. Every day the bank opens and deposits all payments received and forwards copies of every payment to the company for posting. Under a lockbox arrangement, employees should never have access to customer payments; therefore, the risk of diverting funds is relatively low. However, the cost of a lockbox arrangement is often prohibitive, especially for a small business. Although the benefits of the lockbox would outweigh the cost, I seldom find a lockbox arrangement within a small business.

Customers who remit their payments electronically to you also remove employee access to the funds. The payments are automatically deposited directly into the company's bank account, and an owner or designated individual should monitor the account activity to identify when payments are received. In my experience, the trend seems to be moving more and more toward businesses remitting payments electronically to reduce the number of checks they are processing.

Beyond a lockbox and electronic payments, most companies physically receive checks for all other customer payments.

Here is where employees have the most access or opportunity to divert customer payments. Starting with the physical receipt of the check, including retrieving the post office box contents and opening the daily mail, you should have a process to identify how much in customer payments is received each and every day. Ideally the individual opening the mail and receiving payments should list the payments received or simply add them for a total amount received. That individual should be independent of any employees who process the bank deposits as well as the employee who posts payments to customer accounts within the accounts receivable system. All payments received should be stamped "for deposit only" upon receipt, and copies of all receipts should be made to support the daily deposit batches.

The payment listing or total amount received should be forwarded to an owner or designated individual, along with the actual payments (already endorsed) for depositing. The payment copies should be forwarded to the individuals responsible for posting payments to customer accounts. The deposit slip should be prepared for the day's deposit (in duplicate), and the deposit should be delivered to the bank. As will be discussed in Chapter 8, Electronic Banking, new measures can be implemented to complete bank deposits right from the company without having to physically go to a bank branch.

The deposit receipts from the bank should be returned to the owner or designated individual for comparing to the listing or total payments received as well as to the duplicate deposit slips. Once the payments are posted to the accounts receivable system, a posting journal or report should be generated, and the total posted payments should be matched or reconciled to the listing or total payments received and the deposit receipts. This three-way triangular reconciliation among the amount received, deposited, and posted is the only means to ensure that every payment received was actually posted and deposited.

In addition to completing this triangular reconciliation on a daily basis, the listing or total payments received for each day during the month should be compared to the total payments posted for the month as well as to the total deposits per the bank statement for the month. These amounts should agree, or reconciling items should be identified to explain and support any differences.

Case Study 3.3   Bank Deposits Gone Wrong

In our local newspaper, there was a case of an employee of a well-known pharmacy chain who was arrested for embezzling funds from the pharmacy. Since it occurred in the location I frequented, I wanted to see if I knew the person responsible for the theft. According to the story, the employee failed to make 60 days' worth of daily deposits over a period of two months. The story also stated that the branch of the bank the employee made the deposits to was located directly across the street from the pharmacy. My question was, how could the pharmacy not realize that the daily deposits were not being made until 60 days had passed? One would think that it would be apparent after the first one, two, or three deposits weren't made. Someone must not have been monitoring and reconciling bank deposit receipts to sales reports.

I was involved in a similar case where a doughnut store manager was not making the daily deposits on Sunday nights. The policy was that the manager would place the Sunday deposit in a zippered bank deposit envelope and put the envelope on top of a ceiling tile away from view until the store closed at midnight. Then after closing the store and cleaning up, the manager was to drive to the bank

(continued)

(Continued)

branch and put the zippered envelope into the night deposit drop on his way home. To solve the mystery of why the Sunday deposits were not being deposited, the client hired a private investigator to become a regular customer of the shop, especially late on Sunday nights. He did, and he observed the actions of the store manager. When the store closed, the private investigator would remain in his car in the parking lot out of view and continue to monitor the manager's actions. As the manager left the store and drove away, the private investigator followed. They drove to the bank—and straight past it. The manager ended up parking at a casino and brought the zippered bag in with him. The private investigator inconspicuously made his way into the casino and managed to "run into" the manager playing the slot machines. The private investigator spent the next several hours hanging out with and playing the slot machine right next to the manager, watching him remove funds from the zippered bag to fuel his gambling. You can imagine how easy the rest of the case was from that point forward leading to the manager's arrest.

Debit Memos and Other Adjustments

Policies and procedures should govern the issuance of debit memos and any other adjustments posted to customer balances within accounts receivable. At a minimum, a form should be utilized to substantiate any of these transactions. One practical suggestion is to establish a dollar limit whereby any transaction below the limit can be processed by authorized individuals but any transaction over the dollar limit requires approval and supporting documentation.

Case Study 3.4   Diverted Payments Concealed through Adjustments

A local manufacturer with a small staff utilized an accounting system for its bookkeeping needs, including invoicing customers, recording payments, and tracking uncollected balances. While the business was doing better than expected as far as sales orders and production, its cash flows never seemed to meet the owner's expectations. Shipments were processed to customers on a regular basis, accompanied by the supporting invoice, but vendor invoices were frequently paid late, leading to vendor complaints to the owner. The company's longtime bookkeeper worked only part time and was responsible for entering and paying bills, writing checks, posting customer payments, making bank deposits, recording payroll, and reconciling the company's bank accounts. Customer payments were received in the mail at the business and opened by the receptionist on a daily basis. The checks and remittances were left in the bookkeeper's in-box each day, and no other employees were involved in any of her bookkeeping functions. The owner, busy himself with purchasing, production, and shipping responsibilities, came to rely on the bookkeeper for all financial aspects of the company and trusted her, as she had been with the company for a long time.

Troubled by the never-ending cash flow insufficiencies, the owner had one of his administrative employees trace customer shipments and invoices to the accounts receivable system to determine how and when each customer paid invoices. The owner wanted to know if certain customers took extended terms with their payments beyond the agreed-on terms. Within a few traced shipments, the individual

(continued)

49

(Continued)

doing the research identified a shipment that had not been paid but was no longer listed as unpaid within accounts receivable. Further research revealed the invoice amount had been adjusted off the system. The individual brought the information to the attention of the owner for an explanation, and none was identified. The bookkeeper was not at work, so the owner contacted the customer directly to determine why the invoice was written off. That is when the owner first learned the invoice had been paid in full, with the customer providing the date, check number, and amount of the payment. The owner, puzzled as to why the invoice would have been adjusted when a full payment was made, asked the customer to fax over a copy of the front and back of the check from his files.

As you can imagine, when the check copy was received, the endorsement on the back of the customer's check was not the company's standard endorsement. The endorsement area was blank, and the bank that processed the check for deposit was not the company's bank. A review of the bookkeeper's direct deposit form revealed the bookkeeper had her payroll checks directly deposited into her account at the same bank where the customer's check was deposited.

The owner generated reports from the accounting system identifying all the debit memos and other adjustments posted to customer accounts as far back as the system would provide. Several pages of transactions were generated. As the owner reviewed the details, he remembered many of the invoices.

Armed with the limited information, the owner waited for the bookkeeper to come to work. Upon her arrival, the owner called her into his office and asked her to explain why an adjustment was posted to the customer's account when the customer had paid the invoice in full by check. The bookkeeper remained unresponsive as she sat in the chair, providing no explanation. The owner asked her if she deposited the customer's check into her own bank account or a bank account that she controlled. Again, she provided no response. Infuriated, the owner fired her and walked her out of the building. The owner returned to his office and called counsel.

After tracking down as many of the adjusted sales invoices with customers as possible, requesting copies of checks for all of them, fewer than half of the transactions could be substantiated with records provided by cooperating customers. Of the ones substantiated, copies of canceled checks were received for only a portion of the payments. A search warrant for the bookkeeper's bank account information, including her deposit details, revealed she had diverted over $300,000 in checks payable to the company to her personal bank account, all of which were deposited via ATM deposits.

Reports should be generated and reviewed for reasonableness on a daily and monthly basis, identifying any debit memos or other adjustments posted. If reviewed daily, the monthly report should correspond with the activity observed throughout the month. Transactions should be selected on a random basis and traced to supporting forms and documentation to ensure compliance with company policies and procedures as well as to identify any potential issues.

Accounts Receivable

If procedures ensure that all sales are properly recorded and reflected in the accounts receivable system, only three things can occur.

1. Customers send in their payment, and their balance is paid in the system and removed from the accounts receivable (as discussed).
2. Customers send in their payment, their balance is adjusted, and their unpaid invoice is removed from the accounts receivable (also discussed earlier).
3. Customers do not send in their payment, or customers send in their payment but no entries are made to their accounts. In all cases, customers' unpaid balances will remain on the accounts receivable reports, and the company's accounts receivable balances will grow larger and older as time passes.

You should have procedures in place to review and monitor the accounts receivable detail on a regular basis. Ideally the accounts receivable details should be reviewed by an owner or designated individual. Where practical, the designated employee responsible for following up on outstanding customer balances should be independent of individuals responsible for processing and posting customer payments and should have no access to the system to post activity to customer balances. Due to limited capacity within most small businesses, there are often not enough employees to segregate these responsibilities, and therefore it is incumbent on the owner to review the accounts receivable details and activity on a regular basis.

Thefts of cash receipts, sales proceeds, and customer payments have become several of the most common forms of employee theft and embezzlement, mainly due to the ease of converting the payments for personal use. You need to remain vigilant to ensure that all payments due to your company are properly received and deposited.

■ ■ ■

Risks of theft and embezzlement within the sales process are not limited to cash and credit sales. Opportunities exist within credit card sales as well, which are discussed in detail in the next chapter.

Sales, Cash Receipts, and Collections: Considerations

Recording and Tracking Sales	Completed
Create customer expectations (and employee deterrents) by posting signs regarding the expectation to receive a register or system-generated receipt for every purchase.	❑
Ensure that a designated employee is assigned to each specific register, terminal, or checkout area.	❑
Implement a policy that cashiers are not to share their registers or terminals with other employees.	❑
Randomly close out and count cashier drawers, and reconcile the drawer to the activity.	❑
Create a policy that requires each checkout area to remain clear of clutter and personal items.	❑
Limit voids and returns to authorized employees. Consider establishing dollar thresholds for employees to require supervisor or owner approval.	❑
Implement controls to prevent employees from processing voids and returns.	❑
Consider making each employee responsible for his or her drawer and activity, requiring each to reconcile the drawer before leaving, and identify consequences in the event the drawer does not balance.	❑

Consider installing video surveillance over the cashier and collection areas of the business. ❏

Consider utilizing mystery shopping services to report back on the activity within the business as well as to identify potential problems. ❏

Remain vigilant, and monitor sales and the sales process on a very regular basis. ❏

Sales

Implement policies and procedures to allow only authorized designated employees to add new customers, add or change credit terms, or make changes to existing customer terms. ❏

Ensure that employees responsible for shipping product are separate from employees responsible for recording sales, invoicing, and collections. ❏

Reconcile all shipments to supporting invoices within the system to ensure that all shipments have been properly invoiced. ❏

Evaluate controls and procedures to ensure that every sale is properly recorded and reflected within the sales and accounts receivable systems. ❏

Services

Reconcile all services provided to supporting invoices within the system to ensure that all completed services have been properly invoiced. ❏

(continued)

(Continued)

Safeguard the tools and equipment from ❑
  employee use outside of the business.

Require the identification of each customer for ❑
  all parts, materials, and supplies ordered.

Match the identified customers on purchases to ❑
  supporting invoices to the same customers
  within the system.

Evaluate controls and procedures to ensure that ❑
  every service provided is properly recorded
  and reflected within the sales and accounts
  receivable systems.

Collections

Require the listing or total of all payments ❑
  received on a daily basis.

Copy the payments received, and forward the ❑
  copies to designated individuals responsible
  for posting payments to customer
  accounts.

Provide the actual payments and the listing or ❑
  total to the owner or designated individual
  for preparing the bank deposit (in duplicate).

Perform a comparison of the bank deposit ❑
  receipt, duplicate deposit slip, payment
  posting report, and initial listing or total to
  ensure that all payments were properly
  recorded and deposited.

Monitor bank activity regularly (daily) to ❑
  identify any customer payments received
  electronically and to provide payment
  information to the individual responsible for
  posting payments.

Reconcile received payments, posted payments, and total deposits on a monthly basis at the end of each month. ❏

Debit Memos and Other Adjustments

Restrict access to post debit memos and other adjustments to the owner or designated individuals. ❏

Consider establishing thresholds to allow the posting of debit memos or other adjustments without approval or supporting information for transactions or balances below the set threshold. ❏

Generate and review for reasonableness reports covering debit memos and other adjustments posted to customer accounts on a regular basis. ❏

Consider tracing randomly selected debit memos or other adjustment transactions to supporting documentation. ❏

Accounts Receivable

Generate and review for reasonableness the accounts receivable details on a regular basis. ❏

Identify someone independent from processing and posting customer payments and adjustments to follow up on collections for unpaid customer balances. ❏

Remain Vigilant

CHAPTER 4

Credit Card Sales, Transactions, and Merchant Statements

Today most companies accept credit cards from customers as a method of payment. Although it may be dependent on the nature of the business, even service-based businesses and professionals, such as attorneys, accountants, dentists, and physicians, have implemented the means to accept credit cards to better ensure that customers, clients, and patients pay their amounts due. In many cases, especially in the current economic conditions, a credit card may be the only means individuals have available to pay their obligation. While I am not a big advocate of individuals adding to their personal debt by increasing outstanding balances on their credit cards, I am a big advocate of getting businesses paid for the sales or services they provide.

Processing Sales

Even with today's technology, how credit cards are processed varies, from the manual handwritten charge slips still used today up through point-of-sale software enabled to accept and process credit card information. The most common method found today is likely the swipe terminal, where the card is physically swiped, and either a code is entered with the key pad or the signature of the cardholder is captured on the small attached screen. A cardholder's card information can usually be entered manually at the same terminal if the physical card is not present, allowing the completion of the transaction. This is common when individuals mail in a payment on an outstanding balance but never physically appear at the business, as well as with phone sales.

Most frequently, customers sign a business copy of the charge slip, and a copy is provided to them. For manually processed charges, a copy of the slip can be mailed to cardholders evidencing the charge to their card. A growing trend to streamline the checkout process seems to be that credit card sales below a set threshold no longer require the customer signature, and the receipt is simply printed for the customer. While saving both the business and the cardholder a step, it also creates a greater opportunity for fraudulent transactions on credit cards as long as the transactions stay below the signing thresholds.

Regardless of how each credit card is charged, the underlying goal is to accept a payment from a customer, client, or patient, resulting in a deposit into the business bank account. Credit cards are processed through a merchant bank, and fees associated with accepting credit card payments commonly include a monthly fee along with a percentage of each sale transacted. The percentage can vary depending on the card processed as well as the size of the transaction. The corresponding deposit into the business account can be gross (meaning for the full amount of the sales transactions processed) or net (meaning the sales less deducted applicable fees associated with the sales). Gross sale deposits are desirable for reconciling the activity, with the fees and discounts taken as separate transactions on a periodic basis.

Reconciling Sales

Whether you charge an individual's card as a result of an actual sale or you charge the card for payment on a balance owed (as in the case of professional services), processing a charge on a card will result in a sale in the eyes of the merchant system. To ensure that all sales have been properly recorded and charged, it is critical for the business to have controls and procedures to reconcile the credit card activity on a daily basis. Ideally charges should be processed throughout each day, and at the end of each business day, the credit card system should be closed out. The close-out process captures all the transactions processed during the day since the last close-out and produces a report summarizing the day's activity. The report should then be used to reconcile the activity for the day. As with reconciling cash receipts, discussed in Chapter 3, there should be a three-way reconciliation of credit card activity completed on a daily and monthly basis. Sales per the merchant system's close-out reports should be reconciled to the credit card activity entered into the business's accounting system and also to the actual funds received into the business bank account. Once reconciled, the supporting information for each day's reconciliation should be forwarded to the owner or designated individual for review and approval. The daily reconciliations should be supported with the business copies of each charge slip and should be collected on a monthly basis to be reconciled to the merchant statement.

Processing Refunds or Credits

The same systems used to process sales are also used to process a refund or credit to an individual's card. In some business contexts, processing refunds makes sense and is expected on a regular basis, such as with retail sales and the return of products.

However, other businesses should experience little or no refund or credit activity, such as with professional service entities. A refund or credit transaction reduces the sales to the business for the day, reduces the gross amount that will be deposited into the business's bank account, and reduces the individual cardholder's outstanding credit card balance.

Policies and procedures should be implemented to control and authorize any refunds, regardless of payment by cash or credit card. One policy should be that any sales or payments originally made by credit card will only result in a refund or credit processed back to the same card. A second policy should require the completion of a form for every refund processed. The form should require the identification of the individual receiving the refund or credit, the name of the employee processing the transaction, the amount, and the reason for the need to receive a refund or credit. Most retailers require customers to sign the refund slip to ensure that a customer actually received the refund (versus the employee processing fictitious refunds). A third policy, largely dependent on the size and nature of the business as well as available capacity, should require an employee at an appropriate level to authorize each refund or credit. This practice is most apparent at grocery and department stores, whereby an employee can initiate a refund or credit but a manager must approve the transaction in order to complete the processing.

Herein lies the biggest risk with businesses that accept credit card payments. Inherent in every credit card system, whether manual or fully automated, is the ability to process refunds and credits. If no controls, policies, or procedures have been implemented over credit card processing, and if no reconciliations are being performed on a daily and monthly basis, an employee with access to the credit card system could process fictitious or fraudulent refund or credit transactions to his or her own personal credit card, reducing the outstanding balance through the business's credit card activity. The unauthorized refunds or credits, if processed on days with higher-than-normal sales transactions, could be blended within the details, and the resulting deposits into the business account would still remain positive amounts (only reduced by the fictitious refunds).

Reviewing and Reconciling Refunds or Credits

In addition to implementing a process for documenting and approving every refund processed, the procedures over the daily activity from the close-out report should include a review for any refunds or credits processed during the day. Every refund should be supported with required documentation, and the individual performing the review should be independent of the individuals who process charges and credits. Any unsubstantiated refunds or credits should be immediately researched, and refunds or credits processed to the same card number within a set period should also be investigated.

Case Study 4.1   The Lost Art of Reviewing Merchant Statements

---

A small medical practice with two physicians and a staff of five found out how important the review of refund activity was when it lost over $10,000 in unauthorized refunds processed over five years through the practice's credit card system. As with many medical practices, the accounts receivable balance grew, and constant effort was required to send statements to patients in order to collect fees due the practice. At some point, the physician owners realized that if patients were offered the ability to pay by credit

(continued)

(Continued)

card, their collections would increase and the outstanding balance from private-paying patients would decrease, especially if payment was collected up front before treatments were provided. The practice manager implemented a merchant system with swipe terminals and posted signs informing patients that the practice now accepted credit card payments. Many patients began paying their copayments and balances through their credit cards, and collections in this area increased for the owners. Initially a monthly merchant statement was received, identifying the activity processed during the month. As with many merchant banks, the merchant statement became automated and available for downloading. With no procedures in place to independently review the daily credit card activity or reconcile the monthly activity to the merchant statement, the practice grew more dependent on the individuals who processed the charges, recorded the payments within the medical billing system, and generated the daily close-out reports. The practice stopped generating the merchant statement image and simply relied on the deposits that posted into the practice's bank account.

One day a close-out report was left on the terminal printer. The individual processed the end-of-day procedure on the terminal but failed to take the generated report off the printer. The practice manager noticed it and removed it, planning on leaving it on the employee's desk for the next day. As the practice manager scanned the day's activity, a refund processed for $125 stuck out as being odd. Because the office had no process in place to support refunds or credits, there was nothing the practice manager could do independently to trace the $125 credit transaction.

The next morning the practice manager was in early, waiting for the employee who typically handled the charges to arrive for work. Once settled, the practice manager asked the employee to explain the refund. At first the employee explained that a patient had been in earlier in the week and paid by credit card. The patient had returned to pay by check instead and a refund was needed to the patient's card so the patient would not have paid twice. The practice manager asked her to retrieve the underlying credit card slips for both transactions and to bring them to the office along with any other information about the patient and the charges.

The employee went to the practice manager's office but had no slips to support either transaction. She closed the door and explained that the slips were gone and that she had processed the refund to her own credit card to avoid being late on her credit card payment, causing the interest rate to skyrocket due to the default terms on the card. The employee explained that it was only $125 and that she fully intended to put the funds back into the practice to cover the refund. Little did she know that the refund processed would not constitute a payment on the account and that the account would fall into the default terms.

Crushed by the employee's admission, the practice manager left the employee in the office and sought one of the physician owners. After a brief private meeting, the practice manager returned and placed the employee on immediate administrative leave. She was walked to her desk, where she retrieved her coat and belongings, and was escorted to the front door. Thankfully, the other office staff had yet to arrive at work and therefore were unaware of what had transpired in the first hour of the day.

(continued)

(Continued)

The practice manager then generated merchant statements as far back as available on the system, and the paper statements were retrieved from the files. All refund transactions were identified and highlighted on copies of the statements, and a listing of every refund transaction was compiled and sent to the merchant bank to identify the credit cards associated with each refund. More than 70 transactions were identified over the prior few years, most of which were associated with the same credit card number. The merchant bank identified the cardholders as the employee and her spouse. Over $10,000 had been systematically processed over the entire period in amounts below $150, mainly on heavier-volume credit card sale days when the refund could be easily absorbed into the resulting deposit amount with little risk of detection.

Could this scheme have been prevented? Probably not; most systems are built to process refunds without the ability to disable the capability. There are times legitimate refunds need to be processed, and the system has to be able to process them. However, should the scheme have been detected within the first month or two? Absolutely.

1. The practice should have had a process to require a form or some documentation for all refunds.
2. Someone independent should have been looking at the daily close-outs. If a refund was processed on any given day, the individual should have traced the refund to the supporting documents.
3. Someone should have been reviewing the monthly merchant statement and noticed the refund activity, tracing it to the supporting documentation.

Reviewing and Reconciling the Merchant Statement

I recommend a back-to-basics approach to reviewing to detect potential unauthorized or fraudulent activity processed through the credit card system. Much like with the business's bank statements, an owner should receive the unopened monthly merchant statement directly and should review it for reasonableness. If available online or electronically, an owner should print and review the monthly statement. Once reviewed, the owner should initial the statement and forward it to a designated individual for reconciling. Once reconciled, an owner should review the statement and reconciliation for reasonableness and also to ensure that the reconciliation was actually completed.

The review should include refunds and credits processed during the month. For those businesses not expected to process many or any refunds, the review should be fairly easy, as there will be either no refunds or credits or ones that need to be supported and substantiated. Unfortunately, due to identity theft and resulting privacy rules to minimize disclosure of personal information, merchant statements no longer identify the actual credit card numbers processed. Under the old system, it was fairly easy to determine if the same card number was being processed over and over. The latest statements only display transaction numbers, so the business will be at the mercy of the merchant bank if research has to be conducted into the identification of the card number and holder for any suspicious transactions.

This is why it is critical for the business to implement internal procedures and documentation requirements for any refund or credit transactions. The individual charge slips will contain the card number and customer name, allowing easy discovery if the refund or credit was processed to an employee. The first time a refund or credit is processed and identified on a daily close-out and the underlying forms and support are not located to substantiate the refund should identify a problem. Either an employee has failed to comply with the policies and procedures, or it will be an unauthorized transaction. Either way, it should be identified the first time it occurs, and appropriate action should be taken with the individual responsible.

■ ■ ■

Once funds have been received into your company, controls and procedures are critical to ensure that any uses of the funds are limited to legitimate business purposes only, which is where the discussions continue in the next chapter.

Credit Card Sales, Transactions, and Merchant Statements: Considerations

Sales Activity	**Completed**
Determine if the merchant bank deposits daily transactions into the business account on a gross or a net method.	❑
Limit the number of individuals authorized to process transactions via credit cards.	❑
Ensure that the daily close-out of the merchant system occurs each and every day.	❑
Have someone independent of processing transactions reconcile the daily activity to the slips and other records.	❑
Reconcile the daily credit card activity to the daily activity entered into the accounting system and also to the daily merchant deposits into the business bank account.	❑

Refund or Credit Activity	
Limit the number of individuals authorized to process refund or credit transactions via credit cards.	❑
Establish a policy and procedure requiring the completion of a form or other supporting information for every refund or credit processed.	❑
If practical, identify a supervisory-level employee to be authorized to process refunds or credits, and restrict the ability to the designated individual.	❑

(continued)

69

(Continued)

Ensure that the daily close-out of the merchant ❏
system occurs each and every day.

Have someone independent of processing ❏
transactions reconcile the daily activity and
trace any refunds or credits to supporting
forms or other documentation.

Monthly Merchant Statement

Ensure that an owner receives or prints the ❏
monthly merchant statement.

Review for reasonableness the monthly ❏
merchant statement with particular attention
to refunds and credits processed.

Have the merchant statement reconciled to the ❏
bank statement and the accounting system,
and review the reconciliation provided for
reasonableness.

Consider tracing refund or credit transactions to ❏
the underlying forms or required support on
a sample basis.

CHAPTER 5

Purchases, Cash Disbursements, Checks, and Petty Cash

Once systems and controls have been implemented covering the revenue cycle to ensure that the company benefits from every sale and payment received, your focus needs to shift toward the use or spending of funds. Just as sales and collections comprise the revenue cycle, purchasing and cash disbursements comprise the disbursement cycle, representing the second most important accounting cycle in every company. Regardless of how controlled sales and collections are, employee abuses in the disbursement areas can easily deplete your company of its cash flows. Unlike cash receipts, a scheme perpetrated through cash disbursements should be within your books and accounting system, leaving a trail as to where the funds went. However, the trail left behind may not reflect what actually happened, especially if you are using a system that can be easily manipulated, such as the popular QuickBooks system. More discussions regarding safeguarding your systems and the integrity of your data are provided in Chapter 13, Safeguarding Your Bookkeeping or Accounting Systems.

Case Study 5.1   What's in Your Bank Statements?

The business manager for a contractor was responsible for all aspects of the finances for the business. Together with an assistant, she processed all the transactions for the business, including all the billing and disbursements for all the jobs in process. The owners were careful not to delegate their check-signing authority to either individual and signed the checks only after reviewing the attached supporting invoices. In order to continue the finances without interruption in their absence, the owners acquired signature stamps, which allowed them to facilitate their signing of checks faster, creating more time to devote to their jobs in process as well as bidding on new jobs. The owners maintained their signature stamps in their unlocked desk drawer, fully knowing that the business manager and her assistant knew where they were located. Week after week the business manager would meet with an owner to have checks signed, and the business manager prepared accounting reports reflecting the month's activity monthly. The owners would meet with the business manager to review the results, and over time, the business was losing money month after month. At one point when funds were nearly depleted, the company laid off several employees in a cost-saving measure and took other cost-saving measures to keep positive cash flows within the company.

Each month the bank statement was received and copied by the business manager. She then provided the copy to the assistant for reconciling within the accounting system. The business manager retained the canceled checks, requiring the assistant to clear checks from the list of canceled checks on the bank statement.

After a few years of losing money, the owners finally solicited a consultant's assistance to determine how to better run the company to improve the cash flows and profitability. Reports were generated and costs were identified, along with the profitability of each project. While not a banner performance, nothing glaring was identified. Recommendations for improvement were provided, but even after implementing the changes, the cash flows remained poor.

One afternoon when the business manager was out, one of the owners received the mail. In the mail was a bank statement for the business. The owner opened the statement and reviewed the activity including the canceled checks. What he discovered took his breath away.

Three checks payable to the business manager totaling $10,000 were included with the canceled checks, all written outside of the regular payroll process. The business manager was paid through direct deposit. The owner brought the statement to the attention of the other owner, and they contacted counsel to determine what they should do next. Not knowing whether the assistant was involved in this scheme, the owners decided to have the matter researched without either employee's knowledge.

That evening, disbursement reports were generated from the system, searching for all checks written to the business manager or the assistant. None were found. Next the owners researched how these three checks had been posted to the system; all three were in fact posted with the correct dates and amounts. However, the payees for each check reflected vendors commonly used by the business. Each check was posted to a different job in progress, so as not to raise any red flags with cost overruns on any one job.

(continued)

(Continued)

The owners searched for all the previous month's bank statements and located the statements but not the canceled checks. Attached to the monthly reconciliations were the statement copies provided to the assistant.

Counsel advised the owners to place the business manager on administrative leave. On the morning of her return to work, they confronted her about the checks. She sat in silence and refused to answer any of their questions. As counseled, they walked her out of the building and secured her work areas.

Knowing the company's accounting records didn't reflect the transactions that had actually transpired, the owners contacted the police to initiate a criminal case against the business manager. In order to minimize the costs to the company to determine the extent of the crime committed against it, the owners worked with the police to request copies of the bank statements and canceled checks for the business bank account for a four-year period. Had the owners requested the information themselves, it would have been a very costly endeavor due to the bank's charges for the research and copies.

Within a few weeks, the detective called to indicate that the records had been received. Copies were made for the owners, and by simply sorting and reviewing the transactions and activity, it was easy to identify all the checks made payable to the business manager. A total of 155 checks were identified payable to her, totaling more than $750,000.

Once the information was received, the owners worked with the police to put the case together against the business manager, and she was arrested. The owners then determined what likely happened with her scheme. All checks paid by the company were computer generated, and there were no manual checks. The business manager entered fictitious invoices using common vendors whose activity would easily conceal the extra checks. Then, in performing the check runs, she determined where in the batch each check would fall, and substituted blank paper for the actual check stock for those checks. When the checks were generated and printed, the system would think each check printed based on the information entered for payment. The company's system—and virtually every system in existence—would have no way of knowing blank paper was substituted for check stock. The check run would be posted to the general ledger, posting the false payee information. The business manager now had blank checks that could be written to anyone. As long as she maintained the date and amount, the canceled check listing would mirror what was in the system for reconciling.

The business manager then typed each check payable to herself and deposited the checks into her bank account. She utilized the signature stamps of the owners, eliminating the need to forge their signatures. At the beginning of each month, she would remove the canceled checks from the bank statement, eliminating any means for someone to detect different payees from what was posted within the system. To further ensure that no detection could be made, she copied the statements and provided copies to the assistant for reconciling. Had she not missed receiving the most recent bank statement, the owners may have never learned of her scheme.

Purchases

Before any funds are disbursed, controls should be in place to ensure that every purchase is authorized and approved by an owner or designated individual. Depending on the size and sophistication of each business, the level of authorization and approval will vary anywhere from no prior authorizations and approvals required all the way up through the utilization of a formal, written, prenumbered, multipart purchase order system. In smaller business contexts, no purchase orders will likely exist, and approval is often completed at the time checks are signed. If utilized, purchase orders are never formally tracked and are limited to big-ticket purchases. Conversely, larger companies often require that formal purchase orders be completed, submitted, and approved at appropriate levels prior to incurring costs for all purchases, even if the costs comply with approved budgets.

Purchasing should be limited to the owner or designated individuals. Similar to controlling who can add or change customers, controls and procedures should limit who can add or change an approved vendor for payment. Adding new vendors or changing existing vendor information should be restricted to the owner or a designated individual, and no other employees should have access to add or change a vendor. Any new vendors to be added should be subject to due diligence to ensure that they are legitimate and to verify their addresses. It is not uncommon for a dishonest employee to add a fictitious vendor to the payables system, or change the demographic information of an existing vendor, then process fictitious or fraudulent payments to that vendor for personal gain.

You should also periodically review your vendor list for reasonableness, ensuring you are familiar with each vendor. Each vendor's demographic information (address information) should also be reviewed, paying particular attention to vendors that exist within your system with no address information or with a post office (P.O.) box address. Also sort the vendors by address, if possible, by exporting your vendor list into an Excel spreadsheet, and look to see if any vendors share the same address.

Any of these could be a sign of potential fraudulent activity. For example, if your company's disbursement practice includes generating laser-printed checks and mailing them to vendors in your company's windowed envelopes, how would a vendor payment be mailed if the vendor's address information was not included in your system (i.e., there would be no address showing through the envelope's window to direct the delivery)? Dishonest employees often use P.O. boxes to control where fraudulent checks are mailed, and two or more vendors with the same address may be a sign that a dishonest employee has multiple fictitious vendors. It is not uncommon for individuals to spread fraudulent payments between multiple vendors to prevent flagging any one vendor, often with the checks being mailed to the same address (maintaining multiple mail addresses is much harder and more time intensive than simply using one address).

If practical, every invoice subject to payment should be reviewed and approved prior to checks being generated. However, in most small business settings, invoices are reviewed and approved simultaneously to the signing of the checks. If the former is practical, all invoices received for payment should be forwarded to an owner or a designated individual for review and approval. Once approved, the invoices should be stamped and initialed to indicate approval. The invoices should then be forwarded for entry into accounts payable. In the latter process, the supporting invoices should accompany every check to be signed, which is discussed in much more detail in the next section, "Cash Disbursements/Checks."

You should establish purchasing thresholds, whereby transactions below the dollar threshold do not require formal approval and documentation, but transactions greater than the threshold require approval and documentation prior to incurring the cost. The dollar limit should be set at a practical level to avoid constant approval yet low enough to limit the company's exposure to fraudulent disbursements by a dishonest employee.

Case Study 5.2   Odd Individual, Odd Name, and Odd Behavior

The director of the information technologies (IT) department was a bit odd, according to the owners and other employees, and had an unusual name. He also had a very unusual nickname that he used more than his actual name. Although odd, nothing in his actions indicated that he was doing anything wrong or unlawful within the company. Company policies required all purchases to be approved in advance prior to incurring the costs, and every department but IT adhered to the policy. The IT director never completed purchase orders and simply ordered machines, software, and supplies as needed. It is not uncommon for owners, management, and other employees to not know or understand what the IT department does, sometimes by design and sometimes due to the complexities of the systems utilized within the company. The IT director also approved all his own IT invoices, initialing them before forwarding them to accounting for payment.

At the recommendation of the outside accountants, the owners instructed the accounting staff to conduct a physical inventory of the computer equipment, using the last known listing of equipment and the last few years' IT invoices to identify what equipment should be on hand. The IT invoices were retrieved from the files, and any purchased item over $250 was added to the latest listing, creating the starting point for their inventory.

When the accounting staff went to locate the workstations and laptops purchased most recently in the past two

---

years, computers that should have been on hand and in use were difficult to locate. They solicited the IT director's assistance to locate the ones that were missing, and the IT director provided explanations as to where they were. However, the accounting staff was unable to physically locate them or corroborate what he provided.

In reviewing the invoices for the computer and laptop purchases, the vendor was a small computer company using a P.O. box for an address. The invoices themselves were generic forms without color, logos, or anything one would expect to find on a typical company's invoices, and were easily recognizable as QuickBooks invoices.

The accounting staff brought these issues to the owner's attention, and the owner contacted the post office to determine who owned the P.O. box. The individual working at the post office indicated that the owner would have to speak with the postmaster, who was not in at that time, and that the owner should call back later. The owner reviewed the invoices and asked the accounting staff to retrieve the canceled checks for each payment made to the computer supplier. The accounting staff returned with the canceled checks within a day or so and showed the owner that each check payable to the computer supplier was manually endorsed by an individual rather than by the company. Even more interesting was the fact that each endorsement included the IT director's very unusual nickname.

Busted. The IT director clearly had established the fictitious vendor and endorsed the checks to himself. This likely explained why the IT director did not adhere to the company policies regarding purchase orders. The owner called the postmaster, only to learn the P.O. box had been closed the

(continued)

(Continued)

day after the accounting staff started their inventory process. Although the postmaster could not divulge the ownership of the P.O. box, it was clear to everyone that the owner had to be the IT director.

A total of over $50,000 in fraudulent invoices was paid to the fictitious vendor created by the IT director. The owner confronted the IT director with the information. The man tried to explain that he established the company to get the best deals on equipment for the business and that the fictitious supplier simply purchased the equipment from manufacturers and passed them through to the company. The IT director would not discuss the P.O. box or why, if the supplier relationship he established for the company's benefit was legitimate, the P.O. box had been recently closed, preventing any future business deals with the supplier. The owner asked the IT director to take him around and show him every workstation and laptop on the accounting staff's listing. They were unable to find the same computers the accounting staff failed to find, mainly the newest computers purchased, so the owner terminated the IT director and called counsel.

Cash Disbursements/Checks

Policies and procedures over the actual generating and signing of company checks are the most important controls to prevent and detect employee thefts and embezzlements. Starting with the check stock itself, it is not uncommon to find small businesses continuing to write manual checks and maintain a manual journal as the bookkeeping system. Companies following this practice should seriously consider buying a computer and automating the accounting to a package such as QuickBooks. Regardless of whether the manual records are continued, or if an automated system is used, the first thing to ensure is that the actual check stock (and checkbook, if manual) is locked up with access restricted to only the owners and designated individuals. Checks should not be left in a box on a shelf, in a drawer, or in the bottom tray of the laser printer. Checks need to be locked up when not in use. The same policy should cover any voided or spoiled checks and the actual bank statements. These should all be secured with access restricted.

With the increase in counterfeit checks, identity theft, and other financial crimes directed toward stealing money from bank accounts, leaving checks or any other information outside of secured areas could lead to your accounts being violated. Employees, customers, vendors, and visitors walking through the company could observe confidential financial information left unattended on a desk, shelf, or printer. Individuals coming into the company after hours, such as cleaning people, could have access to confidential company and banking information left unsecured. Proprietary business information, such as customer lists, contracts, employee lists, and bids, could also be accessed if left unattended.

It is not uncommon for a dishonest individual to contact an employee or cleaning person and offer money in exchange for access to confidential information. The individual may want to steal funds from the company's bank account through the issuance of counterfeit checks or other means, or a competitor may want proprietary information, such as customer and employee information, to poach either away to its business. Copies are not even needed with today's technology. Dishonest individuals could simply take pictures of information using their cell phones and transmit their photos within seconds. It happens!

You can't control the backgrounds of individuals who come into your business, or whether they have strong enough morals to decline such offers made in return for financial compensation. But you can control what unauthorized individuals see and have access to, especially during times when no one else is there (i.e., at night when cleaning occurs).

Lock everything up, and have a policy that nothing confidential, financial, or proprietary is left out on desks, shelves, or any other area when unattended. Lock shred boxes and bins to prevent access to any information intended to be destroyed. Nothing confidential, financial, or proprietary should be thrown away; rather, everything should be shredded.

Your check stock could be computer forms, and while continuous sheet-fed checks still exist, more common in small businesses are the laser format, voucher-style checks which include a check, voucher, and remittance stub on each sheet. Single-part checks are the most common forms found, although many systems can accommodate two-part laser checks (white and yellow). Most companies that use the voucher style (three-section) checks should have no need for two-part checks, as the stub can be attached to the paid invoices to show that the invoice has been paid.

Your company's policies should prohibit manual, handwritten checks (unless all checks are handwritten), and require that every check is generated and printed through the accounting system. Checks payable to "Cash" and blank checks provided in advance of expenses (advances) should also be prohibited. Further, you should require that all payments be made by check except for petty cash and credit card purchases, and should prohibit the paying of any expenses in cash from the registers or drawers.

Supporting invoices and receipts should accompany every check to be signed, allowing the signer to review and approve each check signed. Each check should be manually signed by an owner, and in most businesses, the check signing should never be delegated to anyone below the owner level. To limit risk and exposure to the company, consider adopting a threshold for requiring dual signatures, if multiple owners exist. Checks below the threshold would require one signature, and any checks over the threshold would require two authorized manual signatures. No signature stamps, plates, or other devices should exist to apply signatures to checks, and the same supporting information should be provided to the second signer for those checks requiring a second signature.

For larger operations with higher check volumes, software and hardware solutions exist to automate check signing. Typically the solution resides between the accounting system and the printing of the checks, and includes controls to prevent unauthorized individuals from processing checks with signatures. The controls may be user IDs and password requirements of authorized owners to release the checks for signing, or may be physical controls, such as a key to be inserted into the device to allow the checks to print with signatures. Regardless of the solution used, the owners or designated signers should maintain control over their access (password or key) and never allow anyone the use of their access.

Case Study 5.3   Automating with Control

In reviewing the controls and procedures of a local company, I learned that the business processed a large number of checks each month and that the owner had implemented a system to automate his signing of every check, creating more time for him to devote to efforts in other business areas. I listened to his explanation of how the system worked and

(continued)

(Continued)

the controls he had implemented to ensure that he controlled every check leaving his company, and I listened to the accounting staff's description of a typical weekly check run. Unbeknownst to both the owner and the accounting staff, I had already observed the device residing next to the laser printer and recognized it. I had also observed that there were slots for two keys in the top of the device, one to turn the device on and one to allow checks to print. When I had observed the device, both keys were installed and the green light was on. I watched the device in the printing room every time I walked by and saw that the keys remained in the device all the time. I found it interesting that after each person described his practice, the second key was removed.

I told them the only people they were fooling by removing the second key was themselves. As I do with every engagement, I told them that I had observed the keys in the device and that it was turned on. If the owner simply wanted to let all the checks print without requiring his involvement, the company should simply eliminate the device, because by leaving it on and open all the time, that was basically what he was doing.

The controls and devices are only as good as how they are configured and used. Complacency led to many of the embezzlements I have investigated.

Unpaid Bills/Accounts Payable

Whether your company is on the cash basis (recording bills when they are paid) or the accrual basis (entering invoices in advance and subsequently selecting them for payment when they are due), you should regularly monitor unpaid invoices and bills to ensure smooth cash flows as well as detect a potential problem within the company.

The determining factor in how you will review what you owe vendors on a regular basis is whether you enter bills and invoices into accounts payable when the invoices and bills are received, or if you hold the invoices and bills within an unpaid invoice file to be posted to the system only when each invoice or bill will be paid.

Under the former method, whereby invoices and bills are entered when received, an accounts payable detail or an unpaid invoice report should be generated from the accounts payable system identifying each unpaid bill or invoice along with the date of each invoice. You should review for reasonableness the amounts due as well as the age of each outstanding bill or invoice.

If you use the latter method, where unpaid bills are maintained manually in a file or folder (common in many small businesses), you should retrieve the file or folder on a regular basis and review the unpaid invoices for reasonableness.

A risk exists that a dishonest employee could simply leave unpaid bills and invoices off the system or out of the folder, preventing you from detecting the full extent of unpaid items. Therefore, in conjunction with reviewing the unpaid bills, you should generate accounting reports (income statement or profit and loss) by month showing the expenses by category. Next you should review the monthly trends within each category, especially for categories with expected patterns, such as rent and utilities. If certain expenses occur every month, then you should look to see if the expenses have been reflected within each month as expected. If there are gaps or missing expected payments, you should then look to the unpaid invoice details to see if the missing payments are within the details. Your comparison of what was actually paid versus what remained unpaid will help you detect a potential problem, especially if expected items were not identified in either area.

Petty Cash

Most businesses maintain a petty cash account for ancillary purchases where writing a check doesn't justify the effort, such as purchasing coffee and doughnuts for a meeting. But maintaining a petty cash account without some level of controls can lead to potential problems and employee theft. Significant effort should not be needed to ensure that the petty cash funds are used for business purposes, and the fund balance maintained should be set to the lowest level practical to minimize risk of loss to the business.

Ideally an owner or a designated individual should be assigned the responsibility of maintaining the petty cash fund. The fund itself should be physically maintained in a secured location with access limited to authorized individuals. The fund should be initiated and maintained on the *imprest basis*, meaning that at any given time, the sum of the cash on hand combined with the unreimbursed receipts should total the exact maintained fund balance. For example, if the fund was established at $1,000, and over time funds were used for miscellaneous purchases, if the fund was pulled and counted, the sum of the money in the fund combined with the reimbursed receipts should equal $1,000.

A maximum transaction dollar amount should be set. Individuals should be required to process purchases greater than the set amount through accounts payable rather than through petty cash. Any use of petty cash should be substantiated with original receipts or invoices. In more formal contexts, a two-part petty cash slip should be completed and initialed by the individual requesting advance funds as well as the petty cash custodian, with one copy provided to the individual and one copy remaining with the petty cash fund. Once the funds have been used, the individual who received the funds should return any unused funds along with original receipts for the portion used. The petty cash slip can then be discarded as the advance has been fully accounted for and recorded. The sum of the funds on hand, slips, and receipts should equal the fund balance.

Once funds are depleted to a minimum level, the receipts should be summarized and attached to a check request form for reimbursing the petty cash back to the original level. The original receipts should be attached to the form, and the check should be made payable to "Petty Cash—Custodian's Name" to prevent any potential diversion of the proceeds of the check. Once issued, the check should be converted (cashed) and the proceeds returned to the custodian to replenish the petty cash fund. If replenishment check requests are received too frequently, your petty cash balance may be set too low, or it may be a sign of potential misuse of funds.

By maintaining a minimal balance, you will limit your company's exposure. Review and approve every replenishment check request. By doing so, you can detect any abuses perpetrated through petty cash early, preventing the perpetuation of a continued pattern of misuse.

■ ■ ■

The majority of disbursements made by most businesses are paid by check. In the next chapter we discuss important controls and procedures for paying expenses using company credit cards.

Purchases, Cash Disbursements, Checks, and Petty Cash: Considerations

Purchases	**Completed**
Implement policies and procedures to limit adding new vendors and changing existing vendor information to authorized designated employees.	❑
Conduct due diligence procedures for any new potential vendor prior to adding or using a new vendor.	❑
Consider reviewing the existing vendor list and demographic information periodically.	❑
Limit purchasing to designated employees.	❑
Consider utilizing purchase orders.	❑
Track purchase orders used, and ensure that purchase orders are used if required.	❑
Review and approve every invoice for payment.	❑
Consider establishing purchase thresholds requiring formal approval and documentation for purchases over the dollar threshold.	❑

Cash Disbursements/Checks	
Ensure that check stock, canceled checks, and bank statements are locked up with access restricted to authorized employees.	❑
Lock up all confidential, financial, and proprietary information, with access restricted to authorized employees.	❑

Shred all discarded confidential, financial, ❑
and proprietary information.

Computer-generate and print all checks. ❑

Eliminate checks payable to "Cash" and ❑
signing of blank checks in advance.

Require checks for payments, and prohibit ❑
paying any expenses in cash from the
registers or drawers.

Require that supporting invoices accompany ❑
every check for signing.

Require an authorized signer to manually ❑
sign all checks.

Eliminate any signature stamps or any other ❑
means of applying an authorized signature
on a check unless other controls over the
check-signing process have been
implemented.

Consider establishing a dollar threshold to ❑
require two original signatures on checks
over the threshold.

Unpaid Bills/Accounts Payable

Review unpaid vendor bills regularly for ❑
reasonableness and for cash management
purposes.

Generate and review accounting reports ❑
regularly showing activity by month to
ensure that expected and recurring costs
are being paid.

Investigate any missing payments or ❑
expenses, especially ones expected to
have been paid.

(continued)

(Continued)
Petty Cash

Establish a fund balance that is appropriate for your business. ❏

Assign a designated individual to be responsible for the fund. ❏

Maintain the fund in a secured location with access restricted to authorized employees. ❏

Require original receipts or invoices for any use of the funds. ❏

Establish a maximum dollar amount for use of the funds versus requesting a check. ❏

Periodically count the petty cash fund to ensure that cash on hand plus receipts equal the fund balance. ❏

Make replenish checks payable to "Petty Cash—Custodian's Name." ❏

Review petty cash fund activity for reasonableness. ❏

CHAPTER 6

Credit Cards and Debit Cards

E mployees may be provided access to company credit cards
or debit cards for business-related purchases. Although I am
a proponent of using credit cards, I am not a big proponent of
debit cards in either business or personal settings. The level
of fraudulent activity within both systems has risen to an all-
time high, and arguably both systems are equally vulnerable
to unauthorized or fraudulent transactions. However, there is a
major difference between the two card systems.

Credit cards are issued along with a preapproved credit limit.
As long as the balance is paid in full each month, the cost of
using credit cards is generally limited to an annual fee for the
account, if a fee exists on the account. Any remaining balance
at the end of each period is subject to interest charges, which in
these economically strained times can be as high as 25 percent
or more. In some cases, the high cost of financing through the
card does not exceed the benefits derived by the small business owner from the credit line, as no other financing may be
available to manage the cash flow needs of the business.

If an unauthorized or fraudulent transaction is processed on
the account, the card owner can alert the issuing bank and
a freeze on the transaction can be implemented. The account
holder can contest the charge and complete an affidavit regarding the transactions but will otherwise never pay the cost

associated with the unauthorized transaction. The issuing bank will have to cover the cost and reverse the charge from the account. In the end, while the account holder will incur time and effort to contest the activity, it will not cost him or her any money.

It is important to note this applies to unauthorized use of the card by an outsider, meaning someone not employed or issued a card by the business. The account owner will very likely be held responsible for any unauthorized activity incurred by an employee or card holder on the account.

Regarding debit cards, although these cards look almost identical to a credit card and are processed through MasterCard or Visa, they are very different. A debit card is linked directly to an existing bank account, and at the time of each purchase, the funds associated with each purchase are automatically withdrawn from the bank account. Therefore, if unauthorized or fraudulent activity occurs within the account through the use of a debit card, by the time the activity is identified, the funds are gone from your account. The bank still needs to be notified as quickly as possible, and an affidavit will be required documenting the unauthorized activity, but the funds will still be gone. Now the account holder is at the mercy of the bank replacing the funds in a timely fashion back into the account. If the account has not been completely drained and there are sufficient funds remaining to meet the cash flows of the business, the return of the funds will result in time and frustration but should otherwise have little impact to the business. However, if the fraudulent activity drained all available balances and the business has cash requirement needs to pay its employees and vendors, a serious cash crunch will be incurred. The only remedy may be the bank replacing the diverted funds as quickly as possible, but in most cases that will not occur for days.

Case Study 6.1   Defrauding a Fraud Investigator

We had purchased carpeting for our family room at a local retailer. Once the order was tallied, I paid a deposit with my debit card. The full amount of the carpet plus installation was not due until the installation was completed, and I indicated I would provide the installers a check upon completion.

The installation went smoothly, as expected, and I provided a check to the installer for the remaining balance on my invoice. No surprises, and we were thrilled with the new carpeting.

The next day I reviewed my bank account activity online and noticed there was a debit card transaction on my account for the same amount as the check I provided to the installer. The vendor name listed was the same as the retailer, but the debit to our account made no sense since I provided the installers with a check. I contacted the bank to see if the debit was made in error, and the bank indicated the retailer had processed a charge to my account recently. Puzzled by the double transactions, and worried all my other activity would bounce due to the overdraft on our account balance, I contacted the retailer. I asked them why they had processed a debit to our account when we had provided the installers with a check. The retailer indicated their policy was to process the balance on the card provided to ensure being paid for the installations. I asked why we had discussed paying the installers by check and why I had provided them with my check. The clerk was unmoved, and I needed to speak with the store manager. I explained the double payment to the store manager, who agreed to correct the situation

(continued)

(Continued)

by returning my undeposited check but wouldn't explain why the store had processed an unauthorized debit to my account using my card. I indicated that the store's policy to process unauthorized transactions was against the law. The store manager also was unmoved by my comments.

Shortly thereafter we had another unauthorized debit posted to our account by the same retailer. This time there was no outstanding balance or reason to process a payment. Once again I contacted the store, and the explanation was that our card was used in error for another customer's purchase. The retailer agreed to reverse the debit, but in the meantime, my account was once again dangerously low and at risk of bouncing transactions. We had to close out the debit card and the account because we couldn't ensure that the retailer wouldn't use our debit card information on future transactions and activity.

That was the last time we purchased carpeting from anyone, and we vowed we would never return to the store for any future business. Unsurprisingly, a year later the store went out of business.

Credit Cards

In most small businesses, a credit card exists for purchases and travel costs. In some cases the card is restricted only to the owners, while in other cases cards are available to designated employees as well. In the most informal settings, one card may exist that is shared among multiple individuals. When the monthly statement is received, someone needs to dissect the activity to determine who is responsible for each transaction. Although original supporting receipts should be required to be submitted, often to avoid late penalties the statement must be paid before all the receipts are received and reviewed. Month after month, the volume of transactions remaining to be substantiated grows, and the controls over the card usage become obscure. The only solution often is to shut down the card and open a new one, hoping better controls and discipline will accompany the new account. The activity within the old card is then lost in accounting archives.

There is a better way, even for the smallest business environments. Establish one credit card account for the business and require the owners to maintain separate independent credit card accounts for their personal activity. Restrict transactions within the business account to business purchases only. The business account should be able to maintain multiple cards associated to the account, with separate tracking and reporting for each individual card. Assign a separate and unique card to each authorized employee, and ensure that the company has written policies regarding the authorized use of the assigned cards. Policies should include a description of approved uses, support requirements for each purchase, and prohibit the personal use or sharing of an assigned card. The policy should also identify the consequences for violating the policies, from rescission of card privileges through termination of employment.

Each individual card should be established with a credit limit to minimize exposure to the business from any one cardholder's unauthorized or fraudulent use of their card. Each cardholder should be required to submit original receipts and documentation for every transaction with their card. The account should be enabled to provide separate statements to each cardholder as well as report on the activity of all cardholders, segregated by individual card. Every month, all cardholders should be required to review and approve their card activity and submit their statements along with their supporting original receipts for approval. Any unsubstantiated transactions should not be paid by the business but should be charged to the individual, as outlined within the company's credit card policies. In addition, the cardholder's account should be considered for suspension until all reimbursements have been made.

Once the credit card activity of every cardholder has been received, it should be reviewed and approved by an owner or designated individual. Each transaction should be supported with an original receipt, and the nature of the expenses should be reviewed for appropriateness and reasonableness. The individual performing the review should initial the statements evidencing the review.

Once reviewed and approved, the credit card account should be paid by the business through the normal accounts payable process.

Debit Cards

Real simple: Don't have any, and if you currently have them, close them out. While debit cards are convenient to use, the risk that fraudulent activity could occur within your account, wiping out your available cash, far outweighs their convenience and benefits.

If you have to have a debit card, and by no means am I endorsing any business having one, controls needs to be established both to prevent (or minimize) risks associated with unauthorized or fraudulent transactions and to detect these same issues as quickly as possible. As mentioned, unlike fraudulent transactions on a credit card, which can be added to the account and go undetected for the month with little or no impact to the business, unauthorized transactions processed through a debit card will have an immediate impact on the business's cash balances. Therefore, these transactions need to be detected as quickly as possible, both to initiate the quickest return of the diverted funds and to minimize the risk of additional fraudulent activity further draining the account balance. The timely notification of the bank of fraudulent activity is the only thing a business can do to minimize the damage once a debit card has been violated. And once violated, the damage will not be limited to the funds siphoned out of the account. The associated bank account will need to be closed. New check stock will be needed, and the change could affect vendor checks and well as employee paychecks if payroll is paid from the same account that has been violated, which is often the case with small businesses.

If the business has activity directly linked to the bank account, once that account is frozen, none of the links will work. For example, if disbursements are withdrawn directly out of the account electronically on a regular basis, for things like rent, mortgage or loan payments, payroll, payroll taxes, retirement funding, credit cards, and sales tax, each and every automated relationship will need to be reestablished with a new account. If any customers electronically remit payments of invoices to your bank account, those deposits will no longer be processed, and each customer will need to be notified with the new account and processing instructions. If the business accepts credit cards from customers and the merchant account is linked to the violated account, that relationship between accounts will need to be changed to the new account. In the end, a lot of time, effort, and frustration will be focused on changing the bank account due to unauthorized debit card activity. You need to ask yourself: Do the potential risks and consequences associated with a debit card outweigh its benefits?

Debit cards, much like credit cards, should be limited to those individuals who need one to perform their job responsibilities. Ideally debit cards should be limited to the owners. If several individuals require the use of a debit card, separate and unique cards should be issued to each person to allow the activity to be tracked by individual cardholder, as with the credit cards. Also, there should be transaction limits set for each debit card holder to minimize the risk to the business of unauthorized activity by any one cardholder.

Just as with credit cards, each transaction processed with a debit card must be substantiated with an original receipt or invoice, and an owner or designated individual needs to be responsible to review and reconcile all debit card activity during the month. Each transaction should be traced to the supporting receipt to ensure business appropriateness and reasonableness.

The company should electronically monitor the bank account activity on a daily basis via the bank's Internet-based system. The owner or designated individual should review the account activity each day to ensure that no unauthorized activity has occurred. This is the best and fastest way to identify when and if the account has been violated, allowing the earliest notification to the bank. As discussed in Chapter 8, Electronic Banking, any individuals other than owners designated to review the daily banking activity should have their electronic access limited to "read only" unless they are an authorized signer on the bank account.

In the event unauthorized or fraudulent activity is identified, you need to notify the bank immediately. This is the quickest way to minimize the activity and loss of funds. If timely provided, the bank may even be able to freeze the withdrawal from occurring, avoiding a loss altogether. The account will need to be closed, and all the electronically linked activity will need to be reestablished with the new account, but the funds will still be available to pay employees and vendors as needed.

■ ■ ■

If employees are not issued company credit cards to pay for business-related expenses, they will need to use their own funds and be reimbursed for any purchases. Employee expense reimbursements are detailed in the next chapter.

Credit Cards and Debit Cards: Considerations

Credit Cards	**Completed**
Ensure that policies and procedures identify and limit authorized use of credit cards.	❏
Discuss with each cardholder the responsibilities of using his or her card.	❏
Emphasize that original receipts and invoices are required to support every purchase.	❏
Specify the consequences if the policies are not followed.	❏
Establish one business account, allowing for separate and unique cards to be issued to each authorized individual.	❏
Ensure that the sole business account allows for individual cardholder reporting as well as an account-wide reporting of all cardholder activity, segregated by individual cardholder.	❏
Establish credit and/or transaction limits by individual cardholder to minimize risk to the business for unauthorized use.	❏
Require each individual cardholder to review the monthly statement and support every transaction with original receipts and invoices.	❏
Ensure that an owner or designated individual reviews the activity of every credit card holder each month, traces the transactions to supporting receipts and invoices, and reviews the activity	❏

(continued)

(Continued)

for business reasonableness and
appropriateness.

Debit Cards

Don't have them in your business. ❑

Ensure that policies and procedures identify ❑
    and limit authorized use of debit cards,
    identify each cardholder's responsibilities
    with using the card, specify that original
    receipts and invoices are required to support
    every purchase, and define the consequences
    if the policies are not followed.

Select one business account for use of debit ❑
    cards, allowing for separate and unique
    cards to be issued to each authorized
    individual.

Ensure that the account allows for individual ❑
    cardholder reporting as well as an
    account-wide reporting of all cardholder
    activity, segregated by individual.

Establish credit and/or transaction limits by ❑
    individual cardholder to minimize risk to the
    business for unauthorized use.

Require each individual cardholder to review ❑
    the monthly statement and support every
    transaction with original receipts and
    invoices.

Ensure that an owner or designated individual ❑
    reviews the activity of every debit card
    holder each month, traces the transactions to
    supporting receipts and invoices, and

reviews the activity for business
reasonableness and appropriateness.

Monitoring Debit Card Activity

Ensure that an owner or designated individual ❑
monitors the bank account activity online
daily to verify that the activity is reasonable
and recognizable and to identify potential
unauthorized or fraudulent activity as quickly
as possible.

Reacting to Potential Unauthorized or Fraudulent Activity

Notify the bank immediately of any ❑
unauthorized or fraudulent activity within
the bank account.

Prepare to order new check stock with the ❑
new bank account number.

Identify all the transactions electronically ❑
linked to the violated bank account.

Prepare a plan to address each and every ❑
item electronically linked to the violated
bank account, to reestablish each item to
the new bank account.

CHAPTER 7

Employee Expense Reimbursement

In addition to employees using company-provided credit cards for business expenses, employees may incur costs or expenses for the company for which they will need to be reimbursed. Business expenses could be limited to mileage reimbursement or could include a wide variety of costs, such as travel, meals, lodging, car rentals, and purchases. Reimbursements to employees may be made under a formal system, such as through the use of purchasing cards, also known as procurement cards or "p-cards," whereby an employee is issued a card with either an available credit limit or a prepaid balance, and is authorized to use it for business expenses. This system is commonly found in larger companies with a significant number of employees distributed geographically across a wide area, allowing an efficient means to control and track employee spending.

However, in the small business environment, employees often incur business expenses and manually submit their costs for reimbursement, which can be done either through payables or within the payroll process. It is uncommon to find a p-card system being utilized by a small business mainly due to the limited number of employees incurring expenses and the cost of administering the p-card system. While desirable, the program administration costs often do not justify the benefits of the system.

Expense Submission

Regardless of the system used to reimburse employees for business costs incurred, two control requirements should always be in place:

1. Every employee must submit original receipts and supporting information for each purchase in order to be reimbursed.
2. There should be timely review of the receipts and supporting information provided along with the reimbursement request.

The policies and procedures regarding employee reimbursements should require every employee to submit original receipts and underlying supporting information for each purchase or expense in order to be reimbursed. This practice should apply to the lowest-level employees, including volunteers within an organization, up to and including senior management and owners. Not only is this a good practice, it is also a requirement of the Internal Revenue Service to allow the associated costs to be deducted by the business. The business must maintain the underlying receipts and support for every cost incurred to support the deductions on the business returns, and the rules apply to all types of expenses, including meals, entertainment, travel, and gifts.[1]

There also should be a procedure in place to timely review and reconcile the receipts and supporting information provided along with the reimbursement request. Employees should be required to complete an expense reimbursement form and submit the form along with their receipts attached. Ideally the policy should state that any items not supported with an original receipt will not be reimbursed. Under an automated p-card system, employees would be responsible for any unsupported purchases, as they would have used the funds from their card for the unsubstantiated purchase. Copies of receipts should not be allowed and should be accepted only as the exception when an original receipt is no longer available, such as when an employee loses a receipt. Monitoring employee reimbursement requests for copies versus originals could help identify a potential issue with an employee abusing the privilege or defrauding the company.

Even with these two measures in place, an employee will not be prevented from incurring nonbusiness expenses and passing them through to the employer as legitimate business expenses. However, the business will be in a position to identify a potential problem or abuse in a timely manner and will be able to prevent the employee from being paid for any questionable expenses.

Someone at the company needs to be responsible for reviewing the receipt details to ensure that the costs incurred are legitimate and reasonable. In the small business context, this reviewer likely will be the owner. Ideally the owner or responsible individual should initial the reimbursement request form to signify that the review has been completed and the reimbursement should occur.

Under a prepaid p-card system, whereby employees are provided available funds on their cards in advance of incurring expenses, employees should be required to complete and submit a form monthly showing their costs incurred, supported with original receipts. A second option is for the employees to use a report of their p-card transactions and activity for the period and attach original receipts prior to forwarding the report to the appropriate individual for review, approval, and filing. The consequences for failing to comply with either method should be an immediate suspension from the p-card program in use. In essence, the employee should be cut off.

Where Are the Abuses?

Employees can perpetrate many embezzlement schemes against their employer through reimbursements. However, in virtually every scheme, there is one common component. The employee submits an unauthorized, fictitious, or fraudulent cost or expense in the hopes of it being approved and reimbursed. In a prepaid system, the same holds true. An unauthorized or personal use of the provided funds is processed as if legitimate in the hopes of it not being identified and questioned. The differentiating factor is the nature of the fraudulent activity. For that reason, a brief discussion relating to several common schemes is warranted. Scrutiny of the submitted supporting receipts and details in a timely fashion prior to providing any reimbursement should detect any of these schemes the first time they are attempted.

Mileage

Employees may be reimbursed for use of their personal vehicles for business purposes. It is very common for employees to inflate the actual mileage in order to get a higher reimbursement or to simply submit mileage for trips in their vehicles that were never made.

Your policy should require each eligible employee to track their mileage in detail, enter their mileage on a reimbursement form, and submit their form to their supervisor or the owner for review and approval. Each mileage entry should be reviewed and recalculated for accuracy. The form should require originations and destinations to allow you to recalculate the mileage using an Internet resource, such as Google Maps or MapQuest. Calculated mileage should then be compared to the actual mileage submitted. Next, the mileage entries should be matched to the payroll information to ensure that the employee actually worked on the days submitted. Last, a determination should be made as to how reasonable the mileage is for each day, given the submitted geographical locations for the day. Given the employee's job responsibilities and the reimbursement request submitted, does the submitted mileage simply make sense?

Your policy should reimburse employees for substantiated business miles up to the per-mile rate allowed by the Internal Revenue Service (IRS). The standard mileage rate is adjusted annually to reflect changes in gasoline costs and other economic conditions. Your reimbursement rate can be lower than that set by the IRS, but if it exceeds their standard rate, the amount greater than the IRS rate will likely be taxable income to your employees.

Travel Costs

Employees may be required to travel as part of their job, incurring travel-related costs, such as airfare, transportation, and lodging expenses. Many schemes exist within these costs. Every scheme should be detected through close scrutiny of the submitted receipts. Regarding airfare, an individual can purchase a refundable ticket for a flight at a high cost. Subsequently the individual solicits a refund for the flight and purchases a cheaper ticket, potentially with a completely different airline. The individual then submits the original higher-priced ticket and profits from the cost difference of the tickets. A good policy relating to airfare is to require the individual to submit a boarding pass along with receipts, so a comparison of airlines can be made.

Regarding car rentals, employees can rent a vehicle for the entire time they will be at the destination. Most car rental agencies now issue the final receipt for the entire period at the time the vehicle is picked up, allowing a speedy drop-off at the end of the period. If the vehicle is used the entire time, there would be no difference in the cost incurred. However, if an employee returned the car earlier than planned, he or she would get a refund for the unused portion of the rental period. In that case, a new detailed receipt would be printed and provided to the individual at the lower cost. If the employee submits the original receipt for the full period, he or she will profit by the difference between the full period and the reduced period. Both car rental receipts will be original receipts. A comparison of actual travel days using time sheets, boarding passes, and lodging receipts should help determine if the trip was for the full period or for a lesser period.

Regarding meals, employees are eligible for reimbursement of travel- or business-related meals, subject to limitations and documentation requirements issued by the IRS.[2] In their simplest state, the rules basically require every purchase to be supported with an original receipt. The business purpose, attendees, and any other business-substantiating information should be written right on the back of the actual receipt. A prudent business of any size should set meal limits to control the costs employees can incur, either on a per-meal or daily limit basis. Provisions can be made for geographical economic fluctuations, such as meals incurred in downtown major cities where costs will likely be higher than in suburban areas. As with other expenses incurred, the submitted receipts should be compared to payroll records and other receipts to ensure that the employee incurred the costs and didn't simply take family or friends out for dinner.

Purchases

The types of purchases employees can incur will vary based on the nature of each business. In some cases an employee should not incur any expenses, as all purchases are made through the company. In the cases of employees out in the field buying supplies, parts, tools, office supplies, equipment, and other items for use on jobs or within the business, employees should be required to complete a reimbursement request form and attach the original receipts. The form and attached receipts should be forwarded to a designated individual or an owner for review and approval of the expenses. The review process should ensure that each purchase either benefited or was used within the business.

Payment Processing

Once the reimbursement request has been reviewed and approved, it should be processed for payment. Reimbursements could be accomplished with separate checks made payable to the requesting employee through the business's normal accounts payable process, or they could be incorporated as nontaxable expense reimbursements processed within payroll. In the latter case, the reimbursement amount would simply be added to the employee's check after taxes and increase the employee's net payroll amount.

Unless the employee is reimbursed an amount greater than the actual cost incurred (which should never be the case), is reimbursed for mileage at a rate greater than that allowed by the IRS (which is not advisable), or is provided a fixed set amount monthly to spend without accountability as to how the funds were spent (referred to by the IRS an a "nonaccountable plan"), the reimbursement to the employees should not create any tax effect to them and the associated costs incurred and reimbursed should be deductible by the business entity, subject to any limitations set forth by the IRS. The three exceptions noted will likely create tax impacts and are therefore discouraged by most businesses' tax advisors.

Requiring employees to complete forms along with original receipts for every item sought for reimbursement will provide you the information needed to review and approve their requests for payment. Pay attention to the details on the submitted receipts.

■ ■ ■

As discussed earlier, the importance of monitoring bank activity online on a daily basis cannot be overemphasized. The next chapter discusses this and other electronic banking issues in great detail.

Notes

1. Internal Revenue Service, Publication 463, *Meals, Travel, Lodging and Gifts*.
2. Ibid.

Employee Expense Reimbursement: Considerations

Purchasing or Procurement (P-Card) Program   Completed

Provide purchasing cards (p-cards) only to those individuals required to incur expenses on behalf of the business outside of the normal purchasing process (i.e., out in the field).   ❑

Ensure that each individual is issued a separate and unique card, with a policy prohibiting employees from sharing their cards.   ❑

Require that employees with issued cards submit a report of their activity on a monthly basis, supported with original receipts for every purchase.   ❑

Review submitted receipts and details in a timely fashion.   ❑

Ensure that your policies include consequences for potential abuses of the card, including suspension of any individual's participation in the program (i.e., freezing the card) when original receipts are not received or if unauthorized purchases are identified.   ❑

Reimbursement Program

Ensure that company policies and procedures address the issue of employees incurring expenses   ❑

(continued)

(Continued)

on behalf of the business and how
employees are reimbursed, including
requiring original receipts for every
purchase and the consequences for not
substantiating every purchase with an
original receipt.

Design and implement a form for employees ❏
to complete and submit for any
reimbursement request.

Require every employee seeking ❏
reimbursement to complete and submit a
form along with the supporting original
receipts.

Regarding airfare costs, require employees ❏
to submit their airfare costs along with
their boarding passes to allow
comparison.

With all other costs, require employees to ❏
write out the business purpose and nature
of each cost incurred. Ideally the
documentation can be made right on the
original receipt itself or on the back, as
required by the IRS for meal costs.

Review and Approval

Review every submitted request to ensure ❏
that each cost item is supported with an
original request.

Review submitted mileage for reasonableness ❏
and compare it to payroll information to
ensure that the individual worked on the
days submitted.

Require a description of the origination and ❏
destination of each trip on the mileage
form. Use online mapping tools to
compare the submitted mileage to the
calculated mileage to ensure that the
mileage submitted is reasonable.

Payment

Once each request is reviewed and ❏
approved, process each like all other
vendor invoices, with the checks payable
to the individuals. The accounting system
should clearly track these checks as
reimbursement to avoid any potential
Form 1099 issues.

Conversely, forward approved expense ❏
requests to payroll to be added to the
employee's paycheck as an after-tax
addition to net payroll. The reimbursed
amounts would be included within the
employee's paycheck and should have no
tax impact.

CHAPTER 8

Electronic Banking

This chapter discusses the changes that have developed within banking and identifies new risks associated with these changes. The chapter starts with a brief discussion about the basic traditional banking methods used by most businesses and wraps up with recommendations to safeguard your business's finances as you move into the world of electronic banking.

Traditional Banking (In-Person Deposits and Manual Check Writing)

The world of banking has evolved based on new technologies and the ever-changing world of computers and electronic information. Historically, bank deposits involved someone physically going to the bank to make the daily deposits, handing the deposit batch to a teller, and waiting for a printed deposit receipt. Drive-through windows allowed depositors to remain in their cars, especially helpful during inclement weather, and night deposit boxes, or drop boxes, were implemented to allow business owners to make deposits at night or on weekends when the branches were closed. Banks required each deposit item to be listed separately on the deposit ticket, and each check required an endorsement in order to be processed for deposit. A big pickup in efficiency was realized by many businesses when banks began accepting a calculator tape of the deposit items in place of writing out each deposit item on the deposit slip. Today deposits can be completed without ever going to the bank, as will be discussed.

Bill payments originated as handwritten checks mailed through the postal system, requiring each check to be manually completed and signed. Each physical check traveled to the vendor, then to the vendor's bank, next to the Federal Reserve Bank, and finally back to the business's bank before being returned to the originating business. Mailing checks created a "float" on the company's funds between the time the checks were mailed and when they were received by the vendor, deposited, and cleared the banking system. The float period could extend from several days to weeks. Once the checks cleared, the actual canceled checks were returned to the business along with the monthly bank statement.

As computers filtered into most businesses, so did electronic accounting software packages. Automated accounting procedures were implemented, and many businesses switched to printing checks through their accounting systems. Today some businesses never print and write a single check; they pay all their obligations electronically, as will be discussed.

Besides deposits and checks, the other transactions common to most businesses were bank transfers between accounts. Traditionally the only means to accomplish a transfer was to write a check from one account and deposit it into the other. With the advent of phone banking, someone authorized on the account could check balances within accounts as well as transfer funds simply by providing verbal instructions by phone to the bank. Today transfers can be accomplished electronically by many means, and in some cases, without approval for each and every transfer, as will be discussed.

The interesting thing about all the banking changes and advances in technology is that many small businesses continue to run their business and complete their banking requirements just as they always have, by writing checks and physically taking their deposits to a teller at a local branch. Their bookkeeping systems continue to be as manual today as they were years ago.

Check Processing and Clearing Changes

New means of banking have been developed that have made their way into many businesses. One change experienced by virtually every bank account holder involved the return of the actual canceled checks. Today few, if any, banks return the actual canceled checks; the ones that do typically charge an additional fee for those checks. I predict as time goes on even fewer will continue to offer this service. Images or pictures of your canceled checks (check fronts only) have replaced returning the actual canceled checks. For those businesses that receive their check images, many no longer receive a complete set of images for all the checks that cleared during the month. Many checks written today by small businesses are converted through the process to electronic withdrawal transactions (processes called check truncation and automated clearing house [ACH] conversion).

As a means of detecting employee thefts, prudent business owners would simply review the monthly canceled checks, especially the information on the backs of the returned checks. Today with images of the check fronts and the electronic conversions of checks, detecting employee fraud and theft has become that much harder, if not impossible.

So what is check truncation, and how would it affect a small business? Check truncation is simply a vendor converting one of your physical checks into an electronic withdrawal from your account. For example, you send a vendor one of your checks. The vendor, as part of its deposit process, converts your check into an electronic withdrawal from your account. Once converted by the vendor, the funds are removed from your account, just as they would have been when your check cleared the bank. The change is that you will never see that check again or an image of that check. Once the funds were removed from your account, the vendor discards your check, and the reference on your bank statement will simply list the transaction date, old check number (sometimes), and withdrawn dollar amount.

Truncation has become an efficient means for a business to deposit hundreds or thousands of checks it receives from customers, as employees can process the payments for deposits simply by scanning each check while sitting at their desks and never have to physically take the checks to their bank.

Case Study 8.1   Where Did My Check Go?

Here's an example of how check truncation works. In Connecticut, the major utility suppliers have adopted this payment processing method. When I mail my check to the electric company, it uses my check to electronically withdraw the check amount from my bank account. I will never see my physical check again, as my electric company discarded my check. The only transaction that will appear on my bank statement is an electronic withdrawal on the day the funds were withdrawn, along with the corresponding check number (in my bank's case). My bank statements don't even list the electric company as the payee for the transaction but simply identify the date, check number, and amount.

The other process, ACH conversion, is very similar to check truncation, except that you typically receive your physical check back from the vendor you paid.

This method works well for many retailers in that it assures them that funds are available in the customer's bank account to cover the check amount, withdraws the funds from the customer's account right then and there, and eliminates receiving bounced checks (insufficient funds checks) from customers.

Here's the problem with these new banking processes. As efficient as both new methods have become for vendors that use them, both of these processes will make it harder for you to detect if an employee is stealing from your bank account, as you will not receive the images of the canceled checks they used to steal your funds. Unlike under the old banking methods, the evidence you would need to detect employee thefts will not be available to you, forcing you to develop alternative procedures to detect fictitious or unauthorized disbursements by dishonest employees.

Case Study 8.2 Here's Your Receipt and Your Check Back?

Here's an example of how ACH conversion works. I shop at a local pet store in my town. When I pay the cashier at the checkout with a check, he runs my check through a reader device on the counter, then hands me back my check, and prints a receipt. The funds from my check are electronically withdrawn from my account based on the amount and information written on the check. The check is simply converted into an electronic withdrawal while I wait for the cashier to complete my sale. I leave the store with my check, my store receipt, and my merchandise.

Changes in Bank Deposits

Similar issues and risks exist within the new processes available to make deposits. Desktop technology along with electronic banking allows a business to make daily deposits right from an employee's desk, saving him or her from having to travel to a bank branch on a daily basis. The new process, referred to as desktop deposits or remote deposit capture, is simply the other side of check truncation (described earlier).

Using desktop deposit processing, a business receives checks from its customers, scans the checks through a desktop reader, stores the images of each check on a computer hard drive, and creates an electronic deposit batch. The batch is reconciled and then transmitted to the bank to complete the deposit. The business retains the physical checks comprising each batch, and images of those checks are stored on a computer hard drive.

The good news for small business owners is that desktop depositing does create efficiencies and capacity mainly by saving the time it historically took employees to travel to and from the bank to make the physical deposits (including delays away from the desk due to inclement weather and the personal errands run during those daily trips to the bank) as well as the time employees used to copy the checks to support the deposit.

The bad news is that a business that adopts desktop depositing without establishing proper safeguards and putting controls in place creates an opportunity for dishonest employees to simply divert customer checks right into their personal bank accounts. Once they have done this, employees can simply delete the images from their hard drive and destroy or discard the physical checks, removing any traces of physical evidence of their crime.

ATMs

Automated teller machines (ATMs) have redefined how account holders access their funds and account information. ATM users no longer need to stand in long teller lines or plan banking around a bank location's hours of business. However, ATMs have also created new opportunities for dishonest employees and new risks for their employers. Employees with access to customer payments can steal checks payable to the business, deposit the stolen payments directly into their personal bank account via the ATM, and in some cases have near-instant access to the diverted funds. This scheme, commonly used by embezzlers over the past few years, simply replaced the old practice of dishonest employees opening an account in the name of the business at a bank not used by the employer. With newly enacted banking laws, such as the Patriot Act, opening accounts has become much more difficult, and thus dishonest employees have shifted to using their own accounts via ATMs.

A second use of ATM deposits that has evolved involves counterfeit, altered, and stolen checks. As with customer payments deposited through the ATM, these checks can also be processed through ATM deposits with minimal risk of detection. In some cases, these items create access to funds even before the bank has had a chance to open and review the deposit items. Unfortunately, dishonest individuals have identified which banks' ATMs create such access.

Why is this important to your business? If one of your checks is intercepted, altered, or stolen and processed through an ATM deposit, the funds will be removed from your bank account before you realize the payment never reached the intended vendor. Although in most cases you will successfully recover your funds, the time, cost, and aggravation involved to correct the transaction will divert your attention away from

121

your business, and you likely will have to close your bank account and open a new account, as your account information has been violated. Changing bank accounts can prove to be very disruptive, especially if you have transactions directly linked to your bank account. Those too will all have to be changed.

Online Banking

Although phone banking still exists today, many businesses have switched to online banking options. Accessing accounts to monitor activity and balances, transferring funds between accounts, sending electronic payments to vendors and employees, and receiving electronic deposits or wires are a few of the new types of activity. Online banking creates efficiencies, saves time and saves money, but it also creates new risks to a business owner. Unfortunately for many small businesses, as they shifted away from traditional banking methods to utilize these new automated processes, they didn't consider evaluating their internal controls to identify new measures they should implement to ensure that unauthorized activity could not occur within their bank accounts. Many have fallen victim to employees taking advantage of electronic access to business funds.

Case Study 8.3   Online Banking Gone Wrong

A local service company migrated from traditional banking to online banking, allowing both owners and the office manager access to the company's bank accounts via their bank's Internet-based system. Although the bank intended to allow online access strictly for monitoring the company's bank balances and activity, it found that transfers between the bank accounts could be easily accomplished through the online access. Initially only the owners transferred funds between accounts, but over time more and more transfers were performed by the office manager (who should never have been granted anything but read-only access). The office manager recorded all the transactions within the bookkeeping system and also reconciled the company's bank statements. Two years after implementing online banking, the owners experienced increasing cash flow issues. After a brief investigation, it was revealed that the office manager had been processing unauthorized transfers out of the business accounts directly into her personal bank account. The transfers blended with other similar transfers on the bank, as the office manager maintained her personal account at the same bank as the business accounts. The company lost nearly $100,000 in unauthorized transfers that were concealed within the bookkeeping through fictitious entries to routine vendors. Should other internal controls have detected the scheme early on? Probably so. But if the office manager had never been granted full access to the online banking, she would not have been able to make the transfers directly into her account.

What Can You Do?

You now should understand some of the changes that have been occurring in banking. We need to shift our focus to how a small business owner can embrace these changes to create efficiencies and capacity within the business without creating new opportunities for theft and more risk to the business. The solution resides in designing and implementing practical controls and measures within each of the areas identified.

First, let me start by saying I am not advocating that every small business run out and implement these new banking methods, seeking the rewards of greater efficiencies, increased capacity, and faster access to your funds. All of these could happen, but you should evaluate changes on a case-by-case basis specific to each set of facts and circumstances. Often the newer methods have costs associated with them; in some cases the costs are significant, greater than what most small businesses likely can afford and also greater than the benefits that could be derived from the changes.

What I am advocating is that as small business owners consider utilizing any of these new banking methods, their thought process includes consideration of new internal controls to be implemented to ensure that the business's bank accounts are adequately safeguarded.

Restricting Online Banking Access and Authority

With manual check signing, authorized signers are identified to the bank through signature cards and other forms. Checks should not be processed without an authorized signature, and banks are responsible for ensuring only checks with authorized signatures are processed for payment.

Most banks offer access to the business accounts via the Internet. The bank initiates access at the customer's request. Consideration must include who will be granted access to online banking, and for what purposes. The issue that arises is when the owners grant online access to unauthorized employees (non-signers) and fail to restrict those users' access and abilities.

Small business owners need to work with their banks' information technology personnel during the implementation of online banking to ensure that only authorized signers are added as users to the online banking and that each user is assigned a unique user ID and password. Unauthorized individuals (nonsigners) can be granted access for monitoring only, as long as those users are also provided a unique user ID and password and their access is limited by the bank to "read only."

Ensure Controls over Check Disbursements (Know the Checks You Issued)

Once checks have been processed to vendors for payment, it will be close to impossible to determine if the checks reached their destination, especially if the payments were fictitious and your vendors utilize check truncation or conversion. Therefore, it is incumbent on you to know all the checks you sign and to know you have seen every check that was processed. As an authorized check signer, you should be knowledgeable about the types of expenses you incur within your business as well as the vendors you typically pay. After a few months of signing checks, you should have an expectation regarding certain payments, especially regularly incurred overhead-type expenses, such as utilities, rent, and insurance. In many cases these payments are typically made monthly for approximately the same amount every time. Once that expectation is formed, you are best suited to identify unauthorized or fraudulent disbursements being processed for payment (check signing). For example, if the electric bill is paid monthly and a payment has already been processed earlier in the month, you should realize when a second electric invoice is forwarded for payment in the same month. The second invoice could be a mistake, allowing you to avoid making a double payment on the same invoice, or it could be an employee attempting to process a personal electric bill through the business.

The primary check signer should manually sign the checks and track the check number ranges of each batch of checks signed. The last check number signed in a batch should be matched to the first check number in the subsequent batch, to ensure that no gaps in check numbers exist. This can be accomplished by simply writing the last check number of each batch on a calendar, matching the first check number on the very next batch, and then crossing the old number off.

Consider Electronic Bill Payments

Many banks are moving closer to requiring customers to process payments electronically to their vendors, limiting the banks' exposure to counterfeit checks and other frauds where banks typically cover the cost of the crimes.

Using electronic bill payments, a customer establishes each vendor within the bank's online system. As invoices are due to be paid, rather than generating and signing physical checks for payments, the customer enters electronic payment requests online. The customer can identify when the funds should be sent to the vendor, and once entered, a batch report can be generated similar to a check register. The funds will be removed from the customer's account, and the bank will send out the payments. No checks will ever get printed or mailed to the customer for these payments.

Most small businesses have yet to adopt electronic bill payments. Any electronic payments made today by a small business are usually associated with payroll, payroll taxes, employee benefits, or some other type of tax payment.

As part of the transition to electronic bill payment, you should work with your bank to ensure that only authorized users (authorized signers on the account) have system access to release funds to previously identified vendors. All other authorized users (not authorized signers) can be granted limited rights by the bank to establish payment requests but not access or rights to release a batch for payment. Only authorized users (authorized signers) should be able to release funds from the accounts, and nonsigner users should not have the ability to release funds from any account.

Monitor Bank Statements

The monthly bank statements should be received directly and unopened by the primary check signer, ideally the small business owner. The primary signer should open and review the monthly statement detail and canceled check images (if received) for reasonableness. In the case of electronic transactions, the primary signer should ensure that all electronic transactions appear reasonable. For example, if the only vendors that truncate their checks are the utility vendors, and the business pays only two utility vendors each month, the primary signer should be reviewing to ensure that two, and only two, electronic payments were processed during the month.

Desktop Depositing Controls

Completing daily deposits right from your business location should be relatively easy for you to control, as the process of remote deposits does not in and of itself create any more opportunities for employee theft of customer payments than making physical deposits at the bank branch. The major control that needs to be implemented upon initiation of remote depositing is a system limitation that no deposits can be made to any accounts other than the business's bank account. The bank's system limitations must prevent unauthorized access as well as prohibit users from adding any other bank accounts into which deposits can be made. If the remote deposit system is configured by the bank's system to include these limitations, the individual can make as many deposits as desired through this process, but all of those deposits will end up only in your business's bank account. Period.

In addition, you should consider how images of the deposit items will be safeguarded on your systems as well as how you will maintain the actual physical checks received once they have been scanned. My advice is to create an area on the computer hard drive or network where the bank's system creates and stores the images, and only an administrator-level user (an owner) is capable of deleting those image files. That way if someone finds a way to beat the remote deposit limitations, he or she cannot also delete the check images from your computer.

Finally, you should consider requiring the employee completing the remote deposits to batch the physical checks by deposit and have the batches forwarded to someone separate for safeguarding. That way if a potential problem is ever identified, your employee could not simply destroy the deposit batches, eliminating the evidence. You will need to determine how long you will maintain the deposit batches as well as where they will be best safeguarded.

Daily Receipts Reconciliations (Limiting Risks Associated with the ATM Issue)

As discussed earlier, you need to implement a procedure that reconciles the payments you receive on a daily and monthly basis. The payments should be reconciled to the receipts posted to your system as well as the receipts actually deposited into your bank account. Ideally these three amounts should be reconciled each and every day, and the monthly reconciliation would simply be a recap for the month. Anything short of this reconciliation can create an opportunity for a dishonest employee to steal payments from your business. The completed reconciliations should be forwarded to an owner (or someone you designate) for review and approval each day, along with the attached supporting bank deposit receipt and system reports.

The absolute best control you could implement to minimize employees stealing payments is to remove employee access to the payments. However, in most businesses, that simply is not practical or possible, especially for retail operations. Most banks offer a lockbox service, whereby customers send their payments directly to an address (typically a post office box) controlled by your bank. The bank opens the mail, deposits the checks, provides access to the funds, and forwards copies of the checks and any remittance advices received to the business every day. Since access to payments has been removed from the employees, there should be little to no risk of dishonest employees stealing these payments. Employees only have access to the copies received from the bank.

However, there is a cost associated with a bank's lockbox service, at times a substantial cost, which is one of the major reasons why most small business owners choose not to utilize the lockbox service for their business. The second major reason is usually attributable to a low payment volume that doesn't justify the cost of this service.

If you implement controls to ensure that all payments received are properly posted to your systems and also properly deposited into your bank account each day, it will be much harder for a dishonest employee to steal customer payments and convert the funds for personal use.

Monitor, Monitor, Monitor Online Banking

Given all the things that could occur within your bank account, it is critical that you or a designated individual monitor the bank account activity on a daily basis, to ensure the earliest possible detection of an issue. Case Study 8.4, which details what happened to my bank accounts and electronic banking while I was writing this book, should emphasize the need to stay on top of your bank account daily.

Case Study 8.4   Accidental Vigilance Detects Personal Bank Error

As I was writing this book, I clicked onto what I thought was the icon for my e-mails. Inadvertently I clicked on the icon that connected me to my online banking. Not expecting anything unusual within my account, as I check it virtually every day, I expected to find the same old balances I remembered from the last time I checked in. Much to my surprise, I saw that my accounts had been drained. Once I picked my jaw up from the floor, I drilled down into my account details, only to find that the bank had processed payments to my online vendors in duplicate. Two payments to every selected vendor had been sent out of my account, depleting my balance. Panicked, I called the bank to determine what had happened. After waiting 33 minutes on hold, the individual started to ask me about my account, then hung up on me (and I wasn't abusive or anything). A second call took 22 minutes to connect with someone and, as the individual transferred me to their supervisor, hung up again. Nearly an hour wasted with no progress. I called a local branch and demanded that someone there start dealing with the problem, or I would close out my relationship with the bank immediately. Twenty minutes later the branch manager called to tell me there were no other reported issues and that it was "user error." She said the funds were already processed out, and if I wanted the funds returned, I would have to contact each vendor and ask for my funds. Needless to say, that didn't sit well with me, so I went to the bank to deposit money into the account so all my electronic automatic withdraws (car payment, mortgage, utilities, etc.) wouldn't get rejected due to insufficient funds. Other than receiving apology after apology, I left the branch with no further information or answers, even though I provided the manager with a copy of the last bill payment confirmation showing that vendors were only selected once. (Luckily I print out my confirmations.) A day went by and I still had no resolution. As far as the bank was concerned, this wasn't their problem, and they were done with this situation.

Had I not checked my account activity, clearly by accident, I wouldn't have known until the next time I checked it that the account had been wiped out—not by some fraudster or dishonest person, but by the bank itself. Time to find a new bank, I think.

■ ■ ■

The next major disbursement cycle in most businesses has to do with paying the employees. Payroll and related benefit costs are typically the largest expenses of most businesses, and payroll has become a ripe area for employee abuse and embezzlement. The discussions continue with the payroll cycle in the next chapter.

Electronic Banking: Considerations

Online Access

	Completed
Limit access to online banking to the authorized signers on the bank accounts.	❏
Require unique user IDs and passwords, assigned only to authorized signers.	❏
Ensure nonsigner users have had their rights restricted *by the bank's system* to allow for read-only access to the banking information.	❏
Ensure the transfer and electronic payment options have been restricted by the bank's system to authorized signers on the accounts.	❏
Ensure predefined transfers between business accounts have been established by the bank's system so that additional transfers cannot occur to any other accounts.	❏
Ensure the bank's system controls have been implemented to prevent any additional accounts, transfers, or changes to be added by anyone other than an authorized signer on the account.	❏

Cash Disbursements

Know your vendors and the payments processed to them each week.	❏
Develop expectations regarding the vendors and payments, such as the average amount and frequency of payments.	❏

Watch for any unusual invoices or check ❑
requests based on your expectations.

Track the check number sequences of each ❑
check run as you sign the checks.

Match the first check number of each batch ❑
to the last number of the last batch of
checks signed, and ensure that there are
no gaps between the starting and ending
check numbers.

Ensure that there are no sequential gaps in ❑
the check numbers of each batch of
checks you sign.

Electronic Bill Payments

Review user rights and access to ensure that ❑
only authorized account signers have the
ability to release any payments
electronically.

Review user rights to ensure that ❑
unauthorized users (nonsigners) have the
ability to initiate payments but have no
access to release the funds.

Review user rights to ensure that ❑
unauthorized users (nonsigners) cannot
change their access levels to grant
themselves rights to release funds.

Monitor Bank Statements

Receive the monthly bank statements directly ❑
from the bank.

(continued)

(Continued)

Review the monthly bank statements for reasonableness. ❏

Review all electronic transactions for reasonableness, and compare them to your expectations for electronic transactions. ❏

Desktop Depositing Controls

Ensure that the remote deposit capture system is configured by the bank to limit all deposits into the business bank account only. ❏

Ensure that the remote deposit capture system is configured by the bank to prevent the addition of any extra accounts for deposits. ❏

Configure the storage of the scanned check images on the hard drives or servers in such a way that only authorized users can delete files from that designated area of the drive or server. ❏

Require daily deposit batches comprised of the batch totals and the actual physical checks received from customers, and have the daily deposit batches forwarded to someone independent for safeguarding. ❏

Establish a policy regarding where the daily deposit batches will be maintained and safeguarded as well as how long the daily deposit batches will be maintained. ❏

Establish a policy regarding when and how the older daily deposit batches (along with actual customer checks) will be discarded and/or destroyed to prevent unauthorized access to confidential information. ❏

Daily Receipts Reconciliations

Establish a procedure to require the daily receipts to be reconciled among receipts received, receipts posted to your systems, and receipts deposited into the bank account. ❏

Establish a procedure to have the daily reconciliation forwarded to the business owner (or designated individual) for review and approval, to ensure that the reconciliation was completed each day. Require that the supporting documents be attached to each reconciliation, such as the bank deposit receipt and the system-generated report for the posted receipts. ❏

Monitor Bank Statements

Ensure that the online banking is monitored and the bank account activity is reviewed on a daily basis to identify potential problems as early as possible. ❏

CHAPTER 9

Payroll Processing

You have employees, and the laws require you to pay them—a cost of doing business. In order to do that, you need to have processes in place to measure and track when they work, how long they work, if they use sick or personal days (for those who receive sick and personal days), and overtime hours, to name a few of the more common items required to process payroll. That information is then used to calculate each employee's compensation for the period, in conjunction with calculating each employee's related withholding and other taxes, to result in the net amount to be paid to each employee. New employees will need to be added to your payroll system, changes affecting existing employees will need entry as well, and terminations will have to be processed in a timely fashion to remove the former employee from your payroll processing. Finally, the payroll will need to be recorded within the accounting system; payroll taxes and deductions will need funding; and the payroll information itself will need to be distributed, reviewed, and filed before starting the cycle over again for the next pay period (which in some cases is every week). That in a nutshell is payroll processing for most small businesses. For large corporations, a similar process is completed, just on a much bigger scale.

Having a reliable payroll system to accomplish all of this processing is key to every business, large or small. Some businesses continue to process payroll completely in-house, possibly using a payroll module incorporated within the accounting system. Most other business owners simply utilize the services of an outside payroll provider to fulfill their payroll needs. However, even with using one of the payroll providers, policies and procedures are still required of every business in order to collect, review, and transmit accurate and reliable payroll data to the outside provider for processing. This chapter discusses the policies, procedures, and measures needed to better safeguard your payroll process from potential employee theft or embezzlement.

Payroll Administration: Adding/Changing/Terminating

Three primary events can occur with employees:

1. You will need to add new employees to your payroll system.
2. You will likely need to update or modify payroll items relating to existing employees, such as their rates and withholding elections.
3. At some point you may have to terminate an employee from the payroll system.

Often these changes are made based on verbal instruction, especially in small businesses.

If the payroll system is not processed directly by an owner, a designated employee is responsible for maintaining the system, entering employee information, and posting these changes. More often than not the same person processes the weekly or biweekly payroll, records the payroll, distributes the checks, and files the registers and reports. There is often no backup person knowledgeable in processing payroll and no segregation of duties within the entire payroll cycle. In larger organizations, there tends to be ways to address these issues, but in most small businesses, it's just the way it is due to limited capacity. That's why small business owners need to become more involved in overseeing payroll, reviewing reports, and approving changes to ensure that a trusted employee doesn't take advantage of the limited configuration by stealing from the company through payroll.

Forms

I am a big advocate of documentation when it comes to employees and payroll, especially when a dispute between an employer and an employee over compensation can escalate into some type of audit by the Department of Labor or your state's labor department. I suspect you have heard similar advocacy from the attorney you use with any employee-related matters. In the case of adding new employees, changing existing employee information, or terminating an employee, I strongly suggest the use of forms to document any such events that require a change in the payroll system. Ideally one form could be used for all three events, with checkboxes available to indicate the use of each form. Include all the fields required for each of the events, and check the appropriate box indicating the purpose of each form. Forms I have designed for my clients to use have included all three sections on the form, one for each action. Whether you create separate forms for each action or utilize one common form to document any type of change, the key is to have a form completed and approved for every change made to payroll. The form, once completed, should be signed by an owner prior to making the change in the payroll system. Once posted to the system, the signed form should be filed in the employee's personnel file.

The implementation of a policy requiring every change to be documented and approved using a form better ensures that every change to payroll will be reviewed and approved by the owner prior to making the change in the payroll system. On the detection side, once the payroll registers and reports are generated or received for each payroll period, the owner should review those reports, looking at all the changes that were processed during the pay period. As the owner reviews and approves all the changes required for the pay period, the changes reported should match the changes approved.

By implementing these changes, the designated employee could still enter unauthorized changes to employees within the payroll system, but your review of the payroll reports should identify any changes you did not authorize. Any questions regarding potentially unauthorized changes could then be traced back to signed forms in an employee's file.

Checklists

The areas of hiring and firing also lend themselves to checklists. When an individual is hired, many tasks require completion in order to add the new employee to payroll, benefit programs, and systems utilized within the business. Alarm codes and keys may need to be provided; user IDs and passwords may need to be assigned; payroll tax forms and withholding elections will be required; company benefits may need to be explained and offered; and other tasks, such as assignment of company-provided tools and computers, may be required to complete the hiring.

Remembering all the items to be accomplished, and documenting that each one was in fact completed, lends itself to a checklist to be used for all new employees. The checklist should list all the required tasks to be completed when adding a new employee and allow for checking off each task as completed. The completed checklist should then be maintained in the employee's personnel file. The use of a checklist will better ensure that every new hire is handled in a consistent manner, prevent tasks from being overlooked or missed, and enable another individual to complete the hiring process and tasks should the primary designated individual become unexpectedly unavailable.

Similarly, terminations often require just as many tasks to be completed, most of which are the reversing of the hiring tasks. These include removing user access and e-mail accounts, changing alarm codes, collecting keys and other company property, terminating the employee from payroll, removing the former employee from benefits, offering Consolidated Omnibus Budget Reconciliation Act (COBRA) benefits, and several other tasks. Relying on the memory of the designated individual can lead to tasks overlooked and not completed and, in some cases, could cost the business unnecessary funds.

As with hiring, terminations lend themselves to a checklist. The checklist should list all the tasks to be completed when terminating an employee, and allow for checking off each task as completed. The completed checklist should then be maintained in the employee's personnel file. The use of a checklist will better ensure that every termination is handled in a consistent manner, prevent tasks from being missed, and enable another individual to complete the termination process and tasks should the primary designated individual become unexpectedly unavailable.

Where to Look for Fraud within Payroll

Compensating controls are commonly needed due to the lack of segregation of duties within payroll, not so much to prevent a potential issue but to detect one within payroll. In reviewing the payroll reports for each pay cycle, the owner should review the payroll register and reports, specifically looking for any changes processed to any employees during the pay period. Here are some issues to look for:

- Unauthorized additions (new employees added)
- Unauthorized rate changes
- Employees restored from "terminated" or "inactive" to "active" status
- Duplicate Social Security numbers used by different employees
- Employees with missing demographics (address, Social Security number)
- Employees using post office (P.O.) box addresses
- Duplicate addresses used by different employees
- Employees with no federal and/or state income tax withholding
- Employees with loans and loan repayments or other adjustments
- Terminated employees not terminated within the payroll system

Payroll Processing

The other area of the payroll cycle relates to the actual entry of hours and earnings, overtime, shift differentials, vacation, sick and personal time, and any other information required to process the payroll and generate the paychecks for each pay period. In some cases time tracking of employees continues to be manual with the use of time sheets. Employees complete their time sheets and submit them to their supervisor or the owner for approval. Once reviewed and approved, the time sheets are forwarded to the individual responsible for processing payroll to review and enter into the system.

Case Study 9.1   Terminated and Continuing to Receive Free Benefits?

During an audit of a local nonprofit organization, it was decided that due to the lack of segregation of duties within the payroll process additional auditing procedures would be completed to ensure that nothing unauthorized was paid or processed through payroll. One of the procedures added was a search for any terminated employees during the period. For those identified, each employee's termination information was traced against information contained within his or her personnel file to the termination date and information within the payroll processing system. A sample of terminated employees were identified and traced, and termination dates were matched between the files and the system. As a last measure to the procedure, each terminated employee was then traced to the health insurance and other company benefits, to ensure that terminated employees were removed from coverage or participation in each benefit program on a timely basis. The audit step revealed that most of the terminated individuals were never removed from the health insurance policy and coverage although none of the former employees continued coverage through COBRA. Month after month, the organization unknowingly continued to pay benefit premiums on individuals who no longer worked for the organization. Should this have been caught by a thorough review of the monthly benefit invoices listing the participants? Absolutely. However, if a process had been in place along with the use of a checklist to ensure that each terminated employee had been removed from the benefit programs, likely the organization would not have paid the premiums in error. The cost to the organization for all the premiums that were paid in error approximated $8,000.

Other businesses have automated the time tracking of employees, from the less sophisticated time clock system all the way up through biometric-based hand scanners to electronically capture employee times of work. Although the time clock may be a step above manual time sheets, the time cards still need to be manually reviewed and approved, then entered into the payroll system. However, for most of the automated time tracking solutions in use, including employees signing in and out on workstations, scanning ID badges or key fobs, and entering codes into a key pad, the time tracking system can be integrated into the payroll system. For these systems, reports must be generated and reviewed each pay period prior to processing payroll. In many cases the times captured need to be addressed for things like missed scans, clock-ins, and clock-outs.

A word of caution regarding automated time tracking systems: Regardless of the system implemented including video monitoring of the time tracking stations, employees have always found ways to beat the systems implemented. "Buddy scans" occur when one employee provides another employee with their code, ID, badge, or login. The first employee can then come in late or leave early, and the second employee can cover for the first by scanning or entering the person's ID as if the person were there. The best defense to any buddy scan scenarios is to consider using biometrics scanners (hand scanners), whereby employees place a hand on a scanner to track their times in and out of work. In recent years the cost of such technology has decreased significantly; for those employees who complain about touching a scanner used by all other employees, place a bottle of hand sanitizer next to each scanner. Then tell those employees that they touch the same door handles in the building as everyone else.

However your employee time is captured in the business, the starting point for payroll processing is to collect all the time for all the employees for the pay period. Someone needs to go through the time specified, verifying the time reported, adding the reported amounts to ensure that the times are accurate, calculating any overtime required to be paid, identifying personal and sick days, and tracking previously used personal and sick time. Once all the time has been received and reviewed, the information can then be entered into the payroll system or, if automated, can be accepted (imported) into the system.

Case Study 9.2 Store Manager Orchestrates Payroll Scam

A tip received by a business owner indicated that employees were not working the hours they reported in one of the store locations and that their manager was aiding the employees in their scheme. The tip indicated that employees would provide their ID cards to other employees or to the manager and then have the person scan the badge in and out at times when the employee was not working. The tip also indicated that the reason for the scheme was to ensure that a minimum number of employees were in the store while other scheduled employees remained at home.

Employees were paid a low hourly rate but were eligible for commissions on their store sales. In nearly all cases the employees earned most of their compensation through commissions. In order to maximize the commissions earned in the store, a minimal number of employees could work to allow only those few individuals to receive credit for the sales and earn the commissions. Employees who stayed home earned their hourly rate. Employees would alternate coming in versus staying home to maximize commissions on days actually worked as well as maximize the number of days they could simply be paid to stay home.

(continued)

(Continued)

The scheme should have been easily detected, as sales were rung by individual employees, and reports should have shown that certain employees working on a selected day received commissions while others working the same day received no commissions. To avoid detection, the coworkers or manager would periodically ring a sale through under the absent employee's ID, reporting some activity for that person. The size of the sales rung under the absent employee's ID was generally smaller than all other sales, to ensure that the maximum commissions went to the employees who actually worked that day.

Since the business did not have video surveillance in the store to capture who actually worked on given days, and since the store manager was involved and facilitated the scheme for the employees, the matter was difficult to investigate and quantify independently. In the end, the business terminated the manager and employees at the store and staffed the store with new employees. Video surveillance was ultimately added to capture and remotely monitor the activity within all store locations.

The next step is to forward the pay information to the payroll provider or, if payroll is done in-house, perform the preliminary payroll process. Whether performed internally or externally, the preliminary payroll should be calculated and reviewed for reasonableness prior to processing the final payroll, leading to the generating of the actual paychecks and direct deposit vouchers. As part of that review, the payroll should be compared to prior periods and reviewed for any changes made during the current payroll period while looking for anything unexpected or unusual.

Once reviewed, the payroll should be processed in final mode. If the payroll is processed internally, the paychecks should be generated and the final payroll reports printed for the files. Payroll taxes are calculated, direct deposit transfers are completed (for those employees who chose direct deposit), and required payroll taxes and other withheld amounts from employee paychecks are funded.

For businesses utilizing an outside payroll service, the paychecks, direct deposit vouchers, payroll taxes, withheld amounts, and all other payroll calculations and funding are completed by the provider. Next, these businesses receive a payroll package, typically on the next business day. Included in the delivered package are the employee paychecks and direct deposit vouchers, payroll registers, and various reports. Payroll taxes and other funding are commonly completed by the provider as well, including any required payroll reporting.

Whether self-generated or received from the provider, the same individual who processes the payroll generally receives and reviews the payroll registers and reports. When this happens, the payroll cycle is complete. There is no segregation within the entire process, and a significant risk is created for the business in that fictitious, fraudulent, or unauthorized transactions or activity could have been processed through payroll with little to no means of prevention or detection. If left unaddressed, such a payroll scheme could continue undetected for years.

The good news is that there is a practical way to address the lack of segregation within payroll processing. When the payroll package is received, or when the payroll registers and reports are generated for those businesses processing internally, the package must be reviewed by the owner (or designated individual independent of payroll) to ensure that the payroll is reasonable. Ideally the payroll package should be received unopened by the owner and reviewed prior to any opportunity to change or remove information.

Case Study 9.3   Were There Issues with My Payroll Withholding?

The same individual had processed payroll at the organization for four years. Week in and week out, all the employee time information was forwarded to the same person, and each pay period, the payroll was processed, transmitted, received, and recorded by the same individual. No one else in the organization ever processed payroll or payroll changes, and the designated individual never missed a pay period. One day during a meeting to review the financial performance of the organization, the designated individual mentioned to a coworker that the withholding on the designated employee's paycheck was messed up and that entries were made recently to fix the withholding. The coworker, finding the individual's comments odd, shared the comments with the controller. Quietly the controller and chief financial officer started reviewing prior pay period reports, only to find that the individual had been overpaying himself for nearly four years. They found that although the man's gross pay was accurate each pay period, he had manipulated deductions from his gross pay and was able to increase his net pay to nearly double his gross pay. In total, the individual had been overcompensated by more than $300,000 during the four-year period. The cost of the overpayment had been spread across different areas of the organization, and the payroll reports generated from the system had been manipulated to conceal the overpayment scheme. The individual was terminated, prosecuted, and sentenced to jail for his scheme. If the man had never made the comment, would the organization have ever detected his overpayment scheme, or would it have continued year after year undetected?

Once the package is received, some of the items and areas to review on the registers and reports for reasonableness include:

- The names of each employee paid during the period are known and familiar.
- The hours and gross earnings of each employee are reasonable.
- The net paycheck amounts (check and voucher amounts) appear reasonable.
- Terminated employees have not been paid past their termination date.
- The hours, gross earnings, and net payroll for individuals with access and responsibilities for payroll processing are reasonable.
- All employees have federal and state (if applicable) income taxes withheld.
- No employees have positive adjustments to their pay without explanation (i.e., deduction fields have not been manipulated to "add" rather than deduct from gross pay).
- There is nothing else unusual, unexpected, or unknown.

Once reviewed, the payroll package and reports should be initialed to evidence the review and approval. Then they can be forwarded to the designated individual for processing, distributing, posting, and filing.

Payroll Tax Returns

Whether produced internally or received from an outside payroll provider, the payroll tax returns should be reviewed for reasonableness each quarter as well as annually at year-end. Review and compare to supporting information prior to signing and filing Forms 941, 940, 1099, 1096, W-2, and W-3. If the provider files the returns on your behalf, review copies of all returns prior to filing.

■ ■ ■

Leaving the three main accounting cycles, other financial areas of most businesses also are subject to the risks of employee theft and embezzlement. Chapter 10 discusses inventory and supplies issues.

Payroll Processing: Considerations

Forms   Completed

Develop and implement a new   ❏
   hire/employee-change/termination form
   to be used for every change to be
   processed in payroll.

Require a completed form for every change   ❏
   posted to payroll, and maintain the
   completed forms in the employee
   personnel files.

Checklists

Develop and implement a new hire checklist   ❏
   to be used to ensure that all items required
   to be completed with every new hire are
   completed.

Require completed new hire checklists to be   ❏
   maintained in employee personnel files.

Develop and implement a termination   ❏
   checklist to be used to ensure that all
   items required to be completed with every
   termination are completed.

Require completed termination checklists be   ❏
   maintained in employee personnel files.

Payroll Processing

Evaluate the vulnerabilities of your existing   ❏
   employee time tracking system and
   procedures.

(continued)

(Continued)

Consider automating your time tracking to a ❑
system that is integrated to your payroll
system.

Evaluate how segregated the functions are ❑
within different individuals for payroll
processing.

Require that payroll packages be received ❑
unopened by the owner of the business.

Require that payroll registers and reports for ❑
each pay period be generated and provided
to the owner for independent review.

Review the final payroll registers and reports ❑
for each pay period for reasonableness.

Payroll Returns

Review quarterly prepared payroll tax returns ❑
for reasonableness prior to signing and filing.

Review annually prepared payroll tax returns ❑
for reasonableness prior to signing and filing.

CHAPTER 10

Inventory Issues and Controls

Prevention: Good News and Bad News

If the nature of your business is service oriented rather than product sales, you are likely not maintaining inventory in the traditional sense (items available for sale). Good news: If you don't have inventory for sale, you don't need to implement controls specific to safeguarding that type of inventory from employee theft. However, here is the bad news: Pretty much every business maintains items to be used by employees within the business, from supplies and tools to computers and other equipment, and controls need to be implemented to ensure that any items provided for employee use are not diverted by dishonest employees or used outside the context of their employment.

Retail Businesses: Items Available for Sale

In many studies conducted, it has been found that retail entities lose more through employee theft (out the back door) than they do through shoplifting (out the front door). One study conducted by Jack L. Hayes International in 2008 found that on a per-case average, dishonest employees steal a little over seven times the amount stolen by shoplifters ($969.14 versus $135.81).[1]

Depending on the nature of the business, the risk of loss due to employee theft or embezzlement may be greater with the theft of inventory or merchandise items than with the theft of finances (receipts or disbursements). For example, look at a business that sells high-volume, high-cost items. What controls should the business have in place to ensure that every item ordered has been received, properly included in the inventory system, and safeguarded until it was sold? In each of these three areas alone there is opportunity for a dishonest employee to steal inventory unless proper controls have been implemented. Employers working in businesses that sell clothes, sneakers, and other apparel have suffered losses from employees who simply put on clothes from the rack and wear them home, often under their other clothes to prevent detection. New sneakers can be removed from boxes in the back and replaced by an employee's old shoes to ensure that the box contains some weight when pulled for stocking. The switch won't be detected until the box of shoes is pulled from the stockroom to be put out on the floor for sale, where a customer is likely to be the first to detect the obviously old shoes in the box. What appears to be a result of shoplifting masks the employee theft.

Case Study 10.1   When Trash Really Isn't Trash

A local chain of three stores specializing in mobile audio systems had a history of losing inventory through thefts by employees. To ensure that no future thefts occurred, the company secured the receiving and shipping areas of each location with locked doors. Access to unlock the warehouse area doors was restricted to the owners and each location's store manager. Whenever a shipment was to be received into a location, the manager would have to go to the loading area, unlock the door, observe the inventory come into the back room, and then resecure the door. With this system, the only means to have stock leave each location was through the front doors, in plain view of all the other employees, registers, and watchful cameras recording the store activity for shoplifting.

When it came time to empty the cardboard and trash for each location, the crushed cardboard and trash bins would be brought to the rear of each store. Once again the store manager would have to open the locked door and observe the employees take the trash and cardboard out to the dumpsters in the parking lots. The doors would be locked once the employees returned with the empty garbage bins. The owners thought the inventory shrinkage would stop or at least force employees to move the thefts through the front of each store where they would likely be detected. In the months after these changes were implemented and closely monitored, the owners determined their inventory was still disappearing from the stockrooms, especially in the main location. Physical inventory counts continued to reveal shortages on the shelves compared to the quantities in the computer system. A review of the camera tapes revealed nothing unusual, and as designed, the rear doors were opened only under the close supervision of the store's manager. No other access was observed without the manager present.

Frustrated by the continued loss of high-end car stereo systems from inventory, the owners decided to return after hours without the store manager's knowledge and watch the store for any unusual activity. The owners watched as the manager returned late one evening and went to the area of the dumpsters. The manager loaded systems into his car and drove away. The next day the owners monitored the manager opening the rear doors for trash removal and watched

(continued)

(Continued)

as the employees brought the trash out to the dumpsters. Once the employees were back in the store and the manager had closed and locked the rear doors, the owners went out to the dumpsters where they found new inventory items, top-of-the-line car stereos and speakers, sitting in the top of the dumpster lightly covered in papers and trash. The scheme was finally revealed. The store manager, a trusted employee, was working with employees, putting their inventory into trash bins, covering the items with other trash, and having the employees take the stolen items out to the dumpsters, only to be retrieved after hours. The owners estimated they lost over $100,000 to this one store manager alone, but they had no real way of determining how much of the total inventory shrinkage was attributable to his thefts.

Controls are needed to ensure that all inventory ordered actually makes its way into the business and into the inventory system. The receiving areas of any business should be secured, with access limited to authorized employees. The rear doors of a business—the access point for most employee thefts—should remain closed and locked at all times, with an audible alarm connected to the door in the event it is opened without authorization. Similar doors can be found in most theaters to prevent one person from buying a ticket and then opening the rear doors to let friends into the movie for free.

New technology allows a camera system to be connected to the same door controls; if the door is opened, the camera is activated and records all the activity until the door is closed and secured. During times when the door remains closed and secure, the camera system remains idle. The new systems minimize the amount of video and disk space consumed and make reviewing the captured video much more efficient because they record activity only when the doors are opened.

Now change the context to a business that processes consumables as inventory, such as a restaurant. The theft or unauthorized consumption of food or alcohol may result in a greater cost to the restaurant than the diversion of payments from food or beverage sales, especially in restaurants where all food and alcohol orders must be processed through the point-of-sale restaurant system, making it harder to divert customer payments.

The context of each business needs to be considered to determine the best controls to implement over inventory. However, regardless of the type of business, all inventory must be ordered, received, posted to the system (in detail within an inventory system or in total by smaller and less sophisticated businesses), maintained until used or sold, and ultimately used or sold. Controls and procedures are needed within each of these areas, or a loss could occur within any one if not every area of the process. The goal here should be to prevent opportunities within each area to the extent practical for most small businesses.

Ordering Inventory

Policies and procedures are needed to ensure that only authorized items are ordered and in quantities that are appropriate for the business. Often employees in small business settings who are responsible for ordering items for the business include unauthorized items or items intended for their personal consumption in an order.

As discussed earlier, even the smallest of businesses should consider using purchase orders. Purchase orders should be reviewed and approved by an owner or other designated individual prior to placing an order. Once the order is placed, the approved purchase order should be forwarded to accounting to be matched to the vendor invoice once received. Invoices should not be paid unless matched to a corresponding purchase order form.

Conversely, if purchase orders are not utilized, orders should be reviewed and approved by someone during the process to ensure that they are reasonable and appropriate for the business.

Case Study 10.2   Acme Hardware: Our Employees Are Our Biggest Problem

When I was in high school, many years ago, I worked at a local hardware store. Another high school student, we'll call him Scott (not his real name), worked there as well. Scott was a year older than I and had started in the store a year before me. Scott's responsibilities included ordering merchandise from the hardware distributor to replace items that were low in quantity or out of stock. Scott would walk around the store on a designated day and use the handheld device to enter items and quantities for the order. Once the order was complete, Scott would connect his device to a phone line and upload his order for transmission to the distributor. A week later a trailer truck would deliver the ordered items in large green bins, and Scott would be there to unload the truck. Scott would also open all the green bins and check the received items against the packing lists. Scott left the items in the bins and had other employees like me stock the items on the shelves.

It wasn't until later in life after receiving specialized training and experience in employee fraud that I realized Scott was stealing from the store on a regular basis through his ordering. Scott would always scan the sale flyers, specials, and distributor catalogs, looking for things he wanted personally. He would add these items to the weekly order and

---

wait for the next week's delivery. He opened the bins to remove his items and mark them off the packing lists as received. The items were already gone from the bins when he assigned stockers to stock the shelves, and he would hand the packing lists in to the owners directly. Scott would often disappear in the rear of the building and parked his car by the back doors of the store. He would hide the personal items in the back rooms and other areas where he knew they would go undetected, and when he parked out back, he would move the items out to his car. The owners were never the wiser as Scott always had an explanation for these personal items if questioned, which was almost never the case. Scott would simply say the items were special orders placed by customers. Because the store used a generic cash register at that time, there was no way ever to trace the special order sales from all the other sales on the register tapes. Unfortunately, the store closed while I was still in college, and the primary owner passed away before I learned enough in this field to have figured this all out. I wish I had, as I suspect Scott stole a substantial amount of inventory from the store during the time he worked there, a period of several years. Although I have no way of ever determining this, Scott's thefts could have contributed to the store's ultimate closing.

Receiving Inventory

Due to the limited capacities of most small businesses and the lack of segregation of duties, often the same employees who place orders are responsible for receiving the items from the vendors. Ideally the individuals who receive in the orders and match the physical items received to the corresponding packing slips should be different from those who placed the orders.

Reviewed packing lists should be forwarded directly to book-keeping or accounting to be matched to vendor invoices and should never be returned to the individuals who placed the orders.

The individuals receiving in orders must be diligent to ensure that the proper items and quantities have been received. Schemes by unethical vendors include sending more or fewer items than ordered as well as substitutions for items ordered, often inferior in quality. Careful checking of received items against the packing lists will help identify these schemes.

For businesses that maintain an inventory system, the received items should be received directly into inventory on the system. A procedure should be in place to match the received items per the system to the actual packing slips for the same period.

It is not uncommon for an unethical supplier or supplier's driver to short a delivery, hoping to avoid detection. Complacency on the part of the individual who receives the order from the supplier will allow the short to be successful. The individual receives the order into the system at the ordered quantity, unaware that fewer items have been received, creating a future inventory shortage when physical quantities on hand are compared to the quantities per the system. The items shorted are then diverted and sold by the supplier or driver.

Recording Inventory

Regardless of the size of the business, the nature of the inventory, or the sophistication of the system utilized, all inventory must be tracked in some fashion. At one end of the spectrum, inventory items could be simply tracked using a spiral notebook and pen. A list could be created of the items typically stocked, and the initial inventory taken. As items are purchased, they are added to the notebook quantities, and as items are sold, they are subtracted. At any time the quantities on hand should agree with the quantities in the notebook. This method would work for smaller inventories with low volume and could be compared daily if needed to identify potential shrinkage issues.

Conversely, an inventory module of an accounting software system could be utilized along with bar code scanning. Initially all items are loaded into the system. As items are ordered and received, the items received are scanned into inventory, increasing the quantities on the system. As items are sold through the sales system, the items are removed from inventory. Reports can be generated at any time identifying items with quantities on hand. Reports could be used to locate and count the physical items on hand, comparing the system quantities to the actual counts.

Without some system to track inventory within the business, it is likely the inventory will walk out, either with employees or with customers, undetected.

Safeguarding Inventory

Keeping the receiving and shipping area doors locked at all times except when someone in authority is present will help prevent inventory from simply walking out the back door. Most stores have this policy, but I am amazed at how many employees never follow it. I often drive behind stores and malls, observing rear doors and receiving areas. Frequently I find doors propped open or doors open with employees standing near them taking their breaks. In these instances there is nothing to prevent an employee from stealing inventory out the back of the store.

Many businesses have installed surveillance systems to monitor different areas, including shipping and receiving areas. Retailers have surveillance systems monitoring the retail space, cash register areas, courtesy booths, entrances to dressing room areas (but not the dressing rooms themselves), and store entrances. Depending on the size and sophistication of the business, security personnel may be monitoring these systems in real time to identify potential issues as they are occurring, such as shoplifting.

Employees can also conspire with family or friends to steal inventory right through the front door of the business. In such cases, employees allow a friend or family member to steal items, or simply steal the inventory themselves and then give the stolen items to an accomplice. The accomplice returns the stolen items through the front door of the business without a receipt, with a story of returning gifts received without receipts. This fraud can be especially prevalent around the holidays, when many people need to return or exchange gifts received without receipts. Most store policies require the issuance of store credit for returns without a valid register receipt, so the accomplice is issued a store gift card. That is no problem for the thieves, as they can use the store credit to purchase desired items legitimately from the business. Using the gift card, the accomplice buys the items and sells them to others at a significant discount. Both parties are happy with the end result. The employee or friend received the items desired, through what appears to be a legitimate means, and the accomplice received cash. This method attempts to keep the suspicions away from the employee yet allows him or her to obtain desired items at a significantly lower price.

A store gift card could also be sold outright at a discount to someone who wants or needs to shop at that business.

Reconciling Inventory (Physical Inventory Counts)

Internal controls, inventory policies, and security procedures are not sufficient to ensure that inventory is properly safeguarded from employee theft. Businesses, regardless of size, need to conduct regular reconciliations of the inventory to ensure that items are not disappearing at the hands of dishonest employees or customers. Formal inventories, typically performed annually as part of a business's tax year-end, include a thorough count of every inventory item, which is very time-consuming. These inventories can take hours if not days and can easily consume the limited resources typically available within small businesses. In some cases inventories are never completed year after year because there are no outside requirements (beyond the obvious tax requirements if applicable) to perform a physical inventory.

Case Study 10.3   Smile! You're on Camera!

One surveillance system I recently learned of incorporated capturing video in response to set criteria occurring within the business. The camera system remained idle at all times, but when a preestablished condition was met, the system turned on and captured video for a few minutes. The same system e-mailed an alert and the video to the owner to allow real-time monitoring of the activity. In the context described to me, the surveillance system was linked to the point-of-sale system. Whenever a void was made through the register for more than $1.99, the surveillance system would activate and capture video of who was at the counter working as well as the customer. The owner would receive an e-mail alert to launch the remote observation of the surveillance system and could watch to see what was happening. The owner said she had caught a number of employees stealing payments from the registers or under-ringing sales for family and friends.

However, it is important to note that although surveillance systems are generally excellent ways to capture activity and investigate potential issues, they are not foolproof, especially when employees know where the cameras are located.

(continued)

(Continued)

One of my clients had installed a surveillance system throughout the office space, which was highly rated space located on the top floor of a high-rise office building. The cameras, which were located internally, covered every entrance as well as what my client perceived to be the most important areas of the business. The camera locations were known to employees, as gray bubbles were mounted on the ceiling tiles. However, a few of the cameras were concealed in a different way, and only designated employees knew of them (or so the company thought).

On one occasion I brought another newer accountant with me to assist on the client's project. Although I strive to provide any assistants a good overview of the client as well as the project, in this instance I brought her to the client's conference room and told her to set up our files and laptops while I sought out the controller. When I returned a few minutes later, I realized I had failed to warn the assistant that the client had camera surveillance throughout the office space, including the conference room we were located. I watched as the assistant's face turned beet red, and that's when I realized I was too late with my warning. Cameras were watching as my assistant had made a few adjustments to her wardrobe that day, thinking she was alone and had some privacy. Too late.

About six months after completing the project, I received a call from the client. She indicated that someone had gone through the office space during business hours, likely at lunchtime, and stole several laptops right off the tops of desks. The president's laptop was among the computers stolen. My first question to my client: What was recorded on the surveillance system, as the entrances, hallways, and certain offices including the president's all were covered by cameras. The client said that while they saw a figure on the video, the person's face was never captured. All that could be seen was a figure going in and out of the spaces. My initial thought was that it had to be an inside job, especially if the hidden cameras didn't capture the individual, and they were positioned to capture anyone in the space.

Even with the assistance of the police, my client never determined who stole the laptops. A significant cost was incurred to both replace the computers and better safeguard the space and equipment. The biggest cost, however, was incurred in response to the stolen data that was inappropriately stored on laptop hard drives. Clients had to be notified of the security breach, and remedial measures were required to prevent any future similar events with client data.

Complete physical inventory counts do not have to wait until year-end. Counts and comparisons should be performed on a regular and recurring basis, especially for high-ticket or high-volume items. Formally, these counts are referred to as cycle counts. Regular counts between the system quantities and the actual quantities on hand are the fastest way to identify inventory shrink issues within the business. Regularly counting and reviewing inventory not only ensures the integrity of your inventory, it also creates a deterrent to employees as there is a strong possibility if they steal inventory it will be detected relatively quickly, initiating an investigation into who stole the items. If the employees see the owner paying attention to the inventory, then they will also likely pay attention to the inventory. Conversely . . .

All Businesses: Items for Use by Employees (Supplies, Tools, and Equipment)

Now shift from merchandise and items purchased to be sold to customers, to items purchased to be used by employees within the business, such as computers, tools, equipment, materials, office supplies, and other items. These items may be assigned to specific individuals, or they could be simply on hand and available for employees to use. In either case, a system is needed to track the items.

For nonconsumable items, such as tools, laptops, and equipment, each item should be marked indicating that it is the property of the business, with a unique number assigned to each item, and the items should be tracked, including whom the items were assigned to. If an item is lost, sold, or otherwise discarded, a process should be in place to ensure that the item is removed from the tracking. Periodically, a reconciliation should be performed, matching the items tracked to the physical items on hand. Any differences should be investigated to determine what happened to the item. The company should have a written policy prohibiting the use of company-provided items for other-than-business purposes.

For consumable items, such as materials, parts, and office supplies, a system should be established to track their purchase, receipt, and use. Once received, these items should be maintained in a secured area of the business, when practical, with access limited to authorized employees. The company should have a policy prohibiting employees from using these items for nonbusiness purposes without prior permission.

Detection

Beyond physically watching your business and monitoring your employees to see if they are stealing your inventory, there are three practical things small business owners can do to detect instances of employee thefts. The first is to use your surveillance (video cameras) installed in high-risk areas and watch the captured footage. However, this could easily be time consuming, especially for the already busy small business owner. The latest surveillance systems that activate only on a triggering event, such as a back door opening or a voided sale over a dollar amount, should address the need to watch 24 hours of video. Further, if these systems send you an e-mail each time the video system activates, this would help lessen the burden of monitoring except when such an e-mail notice is received. Once items are known to be missing, review of the surveillance system may be the only way to determine what happened to the inventory.

The second way to detect employee thefts is by conducting periodic inventory counts, comparing the items and quantities in the system or on whatever means you use to track the inventory to the actual items on hand. Rather than wait for an annual complete physical inventory, small business owners should have employees conduct cycle counts on a regular basis, spot checking the integrity of the inventory tracking system as well as the controls over the physical items. These physical counts and reconciliations should cover items for sale as well as items and supplies used by employees within the business.

Finally, procedures should be in place to regularly review your business activity and transactions for a given period, looking for any unusual activity or trends, such as an employee with higher-than-average levels of voids and returns or with a higher-than-average level of returns without receipts, or a manager with higher-than-average overrides.

■ ■ ■

Beyond monitoring inventory and supplies for employee theft, you should monitor other activity to ensure that dishonest employees have not identified any other ways to steal from your business. One main control every business owner needs to implement to detect a potential problem as early as possible is the review of the monthly bank statement and canceled check images. A thorough discussion regarding the bank statements follows in Chapter 11.

Note

1. Jack L. Hayes International, Inc., "Shoplifters and Dishonest Employees Are Apprehended in Record Numbers by US Retailers" (2009), available at: www.hayesinternational.com/thft_srvys.html.

Inventory Issues and Controls: Considerations

Ordering Inventory   **Completed**

Determine that a procedure exists to ensure   ❑
that all orders are limited to authorized
items in authorized quantities.

Consider implementing a preorder approval   ❑
process, such as the use of purchase orders,
for all orders (or for orders over a set dollar
limit).

Receiving Inventory

Use employees who do not have ordering   ❑
responsibilities to perform the receiving (to
the extent practical for your business).

Ensure that employees who receive orders are   ❑
diligent in verifying items and quantities
received on every order.

If utilizing an inventory tracking system, ensure   ❑
that all orders received are received directly
into the tracking system.

Ensure that the completed receiving forms and   ❑
packing lists are forwarded to accounting to
be matched to vendor invoices prior to
payment of the invoices.

Recording Inventory

Implement an inventory tracking system for   ❑
items to be resold (merchandise) through the
business.

(continued)

169

(Continued)

Implement an inventory tracking system for items to be used by employees within the business (computers, tools, supplies, materials, etc.). ❑

Safeguarding Inventory

Ensure that shipping and receiving areas, and any other doors or points of access, remain locked at all times, and consider installing alarms to those doors to identify when they are being used. ❑

Consider the use of video surveillance systems to monitor high-risk areas where inventory could be stolen, such as rear doors and loading areas. ❑

Monitor for any unusual patterns or trends regarding customer returns without receipts. ❑

Reconciling Inventory

Consider conducting regular test counts of selected items on an unannounced and unplanned basis. ❑

Compare quantities on hand for selected items to the quantities within the inventory tracking system, and investigate any differences. ❑

Company-Provided Supplies and Equipment

Label and number all items purchased to be used by employees within the business. ❑

Develop a tracking system to track each
item along with assigned numbers for
each. ❑

Develop a process to notify the custodian of
the tracking system of any tracked items
being disposed of, to enable timely removal
from the tracking system. ❑

Consider conducting regular test counts of
selected items on an unannounced and
unplanned basis. ❑

Compare quantities on hand for selected items
to the quantities within the tracking system,
and investigate any differences. ❑

Implement a process to secure all consumable
items used by employees within the
business (supplies, materials), and limit
access to those items to authorized
individuals. ❑

Create and distribute a policy that prohibits all
employees from using company-provided
items or supplies outside the business or for
personal use. ❑

Detection

Monitor and observe your employees. ❑

Consider installing video surveillance systems in
high-risk areas, and monitor the captured
activity for any unusual or suspicious activity. ❑

Conduct regular physical counts of inventory
items, and compare quantities on hand to
quantities within the tracked system. ❑

(continued)

(Continued)

Investigate any identified differences in
quantities. ❏

Regularly review the business activity and
transactions for any unusual activity or
trends. ❏

CHAPTER 11

Bank Statements, Canceled Checks, and Reconciliations

As you will find when you review Lester Pratt's book, *Embezzlement Controls for Business Enterprises*, reprinted in Appendix A, some basic controls have never changed. Through automation or delegation or complacency, these basic controls have been abandoned all too frequently, and the business owners who have allowed this to happen have fallen victim to employee thefts and embezzlements. In my experience, far too many embezzlement schemes went on for months and in many cases years before being detected, when the schemes should have been detected in the first month they started. This is especially true in small business environments where the volume of transactions is manageable and significantly less than that found in the largest of corporations.

When it comes to the bank statements and bank reconciliations, I have always had a back-to-basics approach to these items. My position has not changed in 22 years with regard to bank statements. The only person who should receive the unopened bank statement is the owner who is the primary check signer for the business. The next case study shows what could happen when that is not the case in your business.

Case Study 11.1 No Oversight Costs Thousands

The bookkeeper for a small local business was originally hired to manage the finances of the company's owner, including recording sales, processing customer payments, making the deposits, processing bills, generating checks, mailing payments to vendors, and processing payroll. Was there too much delegation to one person? Absolutely! Is that situation common? It's very common in a small business, especially in the current economic climate, when most small business owners are looking to minimize the number of employees to control costs.

Over time the owner grew more and more comfortable with the bookkeeper's work, and as time passed, more and more control was shifted toward her. Although the owner signed all the checks and was the only authorized signer, at times the owner was away and unable to sign checks. At first he presigned blank checks in the event bills needed to be paid while he was away. Later, at the recommendation of the bookkeeper, he simply purchased a signature stamp that the bookkeeper could use in his absence. The rationale was that there should be no blank signed checks around and that checks should be signed only after they had been written. Sounds rational—right? It happens all the time.

The owner initially received the bank statements, but, as time passed, he delegated this function to the bookkeeper as well. Now the bookkeeper had total control over all aspects of the finances for the business, with the owner spending less and less time reviewing the activity, relying solely on the information provided by his bookkeeper and trusting her to be honest. They had become close friends (or so he thought).

The owner knew the bookkeeper was hitting hard times, raising two small children and going through a difficult divorce. She complained frequently to him about her ex-husband and how she struggled to make ends meet without her ex paying the court-ordered child support and alimony. The owner just never considered that she would turn to his business to make ends meet in her home situation.

One afternoon after the bookkeeper had left for the day the owner saw a bank statement sitting on her desk. Not wanting the statement left out for others to see, he picked it up to put it away. As he glanced through the activity, he noted debit card transactions. Interesting, as he had never ordered or authorized one and was unaware the business even had a debit card. There were gas purchases and other payments made via the debit card as well as automated teller machine (ATM) withdrawals. As he scanned through the images of canceled checks, he noted two of particular interest. One was payable to a cellular phone company the business did not use, and the other was payable to the bookkeeper herself. The total of the checks was about $500, and the total of the debit card and ATM transactions was close to $400. There was nearly $1,000 in activity that month alone that he was unaware of. Now he wondered how long those types of transactions had been occurring. He went to the drawer where he thought the bank statements were maintained, the place where they had been historically maintained, and found none.

The owner searched the files but failed to locate the statements. He sat at the bookkeeper's desk and turned on her computer. After logging on, he accessed the company's QuickBooks system. He scanned the bank registers to see how the activity recently identified was recorded within

(continued)

175

(Continued)

QuickBooks. As he found each entry, the nature of each transaction was different in QuickBooks than what actually happened according to the bank statement. Although each transaction was included within QuickBooks, the activity was concealed as different vendor activity within QuickBooks.

The owner called the bookkeeper at home a short time later and asked her where the bank statements were maintained. She responded by describing where they used to be kept, and the owner told her they were not there (a big mistake in how he handled what he found; he notified her that he knew what she had been doing—the jig was up).

She didn't come to work the following morning, nor did she call to say she would not be coming in as usual, leaving the business exposed without a worker in the critical financial position she had filled. The owner went to the local branch of his bank and requested copies of the previous months' bank statements. The bank officer, identifying the owner's sense of urgency, printed as many months as possible from the system. However, the older months had to be requested from the research department. The owner scanned each monthly statement and recognized similar transactions in all the months provided.

Once all the statements were received for the account, the owner identified close to $30,000 in unauthorized transactions within the previous two-year period. The owner knew the bookkeeper had no assets or ability to repay the diverted funds and decided that spending additional funds on professional and legal fees to pursue a judgment he would likely never collect made little sense. He filed an

> insurance claim for the maximum coverage per his policy, a
> mere $10,000, and recovered all but the deductible amount
> of $500 from the policy.

Should the owner have detected this scheme and the unauthorized activity in the first month it occurred? Definitely! How
could he have done so? He could have simply received, opened,
and reviewed the bank statement prior to having it reconciled
by his bookkeeper.

Bank Statements

All bank statements for every bank account should be received
unopened by you, the business owner. Where practical, you
should direct your banks to send the bank statements straight
to your residence rather than the business address, which will
further prevent any employees from gaining access to the statements.

Ideally you (the business owner) should be signing all the
checks and are best suited to review the transactions on the bank
statements for reasonableness. As you should have reviewed the
supporting invoices and/or check requests for each check you
signed, you should be familiar with the vendors typically paid as
well as the amounts that are paid. You should be aware if there
are any debit card purchases or ATM or electronic withdrawals
from your accounts.

Your review for reasonableness is not a reconciliation of the
account to your bookkeeping system; rather it is a scan of the
activity to ensure that no unexplained or unauthorized transactions were processed through your account during the month.

With regard to deposit activity, you should be familiar with
your deposit frequency (daily, weekly, haphazard, etc.) and
compare the actual deposit activity to your expected activity.

You should be familiar with the typical deposits of your business as well as when unusual transactions occur. If any payments are received from customers electronically, you should review for these transactions as well.

Once you have opened and reviewed your statements for reasonableness, you should initial the statements. Doing this demonstrates to your employees that you do in fact review the statements in detail and also provides a critical documentation requirement should your business ever require a financial audit. Then you can forward the initialed statements to a designated individual to be reconciled with the bookkeeping or accounting records for each account.

Investment Account Statements

If you are a small business owner who is fortunate enough to have investment accounts for the business, the same measures hold true as for the bank accounts just discussed. Investment accounts include cash sweep accounts, savings accounts, money market accounts, and pure investment-type accounts. All statements should be received unopened by you, reviewed for reasonableness, and then provided to a designated employee for reconciling to your records.

Canceled Checks

As discussed in more detail in Chapter 8, Electronic Banking, banks seldom, if ever, return the actual canceled checks today. Rather they provide images of the front of each canceled check. Some banks have stopped returning images altogether, offering customers access to the canceled check images through the bank's online systems. The trend to stop returning canceled checks has become problematic for detecting instances of employee fraud and embezzlement. While some schemes could be easily detected on the front of the canceled checks based on the payees, amounts, and signatures, other more imaginative schemes can be detected only through a review of the backs of the canceled checks.

Here's the dilemma. Without access to easily review the front and back of each canceled check each month, do you, the business owner, have any means to detect schemes of this nature? Likely the answer is no. Anything short of receiving the actual canceled checks each month will cause you to spend significantly more time and effort reviewing canceled checks for reasonableness. With the movement toward paperless statements and image access, you will likely have to review each check, one at a time, on your computer screen from within the bank's online system. What used to take a few minutes of flipping through canceled checks could take hours, depending on the number of checks that cleared and the speed of your access to the bank's system. It is for these reasons that I am not a proponent or supporter of the direction banks are taking with their treatment of canceled checks and statements.

Your review of the canceled checks may be the only means to detect these schemes. You should talk with your bank about the return of canceled checks or printed images of both the front and back of each check. I suspect there could be a fee associated with either service, but in my opinion the benefit derived from your review to prevent or detect a theft should outweigh the cost. If the cost is prohibitive, you may be with the wrong bank. Banks that currently return images of checks often send customers the "default" statement—what you get unless you ask for something else. Typically the default images are fronts only, 10 to 12 per page (way too small to review). If you contact your bank, you may be pleasantly surprised to learn that it can send you images of the front and back of each canceled check, side by side in some cases, to allow you to efficiently complete your review. Once again, it will likely come with an additional cost.

I strongly recommend that you look into this issue to ensure that you have the best means possible to detect a potential issue perpetrated through disbursements.

Case Study 11.2   The All-Accepting ATM Deposits

A financial clerk in a local entity was responsible for the cash disbursements area of accounting for the organization. Invoices would come to the business office through the mail, and she would open the mail and review the invoices to be paid. She also matched the invoices to any other supporting documentation, such as a purchase order or check request, if either existed. Often they were not used, and the invoice was all she had to pay the amount due. Invoices were then sent to each department for review and approval and were returned initialed by the department supervisor evidencing the approval. Once received, the clerk would enter the invoices into accounts payable and process payments when due dates were reached. The clerk would generate the checks, process them for signing, and, once signed, mail the payments to the vendors. The clerk filed the paid invoices alphabetically by vendor name, with a check voucher attached showing the invoice had been paid.

As part of the bank reconciliation process for the organization, the disbursement portion of the bank statement was provided to the clerk to reconcile the disbursements. Checks appearing on the bank statement were cleared within the payables system. Once completed, another clerk reconciled the deposits.

During an annual audit, a sample of disbursements was selected for audit testing. Each selected transaction was traced from the accounting system to the bank statement and also to the underlying supporting documentation (invoices). In reviewing the sample transactions, the auditor scanned the bank images of the canceled checks. Transaction after transaction was matched to what was in the system, what was on the bank statement and the canceled check, and what was on the supporting paid invoice.

The auditor noticed that the mailing address on the front of one check was in Chicago, likely a lockbox address used by the national vendor. However, the check physically cleared at a local bank. Curious as to how the check mailed to Chicago could have cleared at a bank in town, the auditor expanded the test of transactions to include many more similar payments, especially to the same vendor.

The scheme was detected. The clerk had been writing checks payable to vendors commonly paid by the organization, forging the signatures on those checks, and processing the checks payable to vendors as deposits into her own personal bank account using ATMs to complete her deposits. To avoid detection by an alert bank employee, she always included other deposit items in her deposits and put the checks payable to vendors in the middle of other legitimate deposit items.

A search warrant served on her bank deposit details revealed she had diverted over $30,000 in fraudulent payments by the organization into her personal bank account.

Bank Reconciliations

Bank reconciliations are another lost art of manual bookkeeping, a casualty of automating the bookkeeping and accounting functions. Traditional bank reconciliations were completed manually right on the back of the bank statements themselves. If you look, I bet most of your statements still print with the bank reconciliation form right on the back.

Software programs now allow bank reconciliations to be performed right through the systems, eliminating the need to prepare manual reconciliations. These are a very efficient way to ensure that the accounting records are reconciled to the actual bank statements. However, even with automation, the reconciliations are helpful only if they are actually completed, reviewed, and printed to prove that they were completed. Complacency has set in far too frequently, and the bank reconciliations no longer are printed and attached to the monthly statements.

As with the review of the bank statements, I encourage you to return back to basics with the reconciliations. Every bank account needs to be reconciled every month. Once the bank statement has been received and reviewed by you, it should be forwarded to a designated individual for reconciling. Whether prepared manually or through the system, a final reconciliation should be generated for each account every month and attached to the supporting bank statement. You should review the statement and the completed reconciliation for reasonableness and then initial it. Then the bank statement with reconciliation attached should be returned to the designated individual for filing.

As part of your review, you should ensure that the reconciliation was in fact completed and that the items identified as outstanding or in transit are reasonable. It is not uncommon to find outstanding checks and deposits that are months and years old, remaining on the lists month after month. Someone at some point needs to investigate these items and address how to remedy each one.

Case Study 11.3   Outstanding Checks: How Long Is Enough?

Recently I reviewed the controls and procedures of a local business. I had no previous experience with the business but met the owner at a networking event. After talking for a few minutes, the owner thought it would be beneficial to have me come in and review how his business was maintained financially. I spent a little more than a day at the business, interviewing employees and reviewing reports, and obtained a sufficient understanding of their processes and procedures.

As I reviewed the latest bank reconciliation on the screen, I learned that the bookkeeper never printed the reconciliations. Month after month she simply entered the activity per the bank statement, marked the cleared items, and processed the final reconciliation, updating the flags on each transaction from uncleared to cleared. I had her print the last reconciliation, the only one she could still access. As I reviewed the outstanding deposits and checks, I noticed that all of the items listed were more than 12 months old. Most of the listed items were between two and seven years old. I asked the bookkeeper how long she planned to keep the items on the lists. She said there was no process to remove or address the items, so they simply rolled month after month. She had been with the company for nearly 20 years.

When I showed this to the owner, he had no idea of what was going on. He had never reviewed a reconciliation and assumed his outside accountants handled these types of issues for him. Now the fun set in: The business needed to determine how to address each old item and how the corresponding entries would be recorded within the bookkeeping system to remove the items from the lists.

Case Study 11.4   How Much Do You Want It to Be?

The bookkeeper for a local business was responsible for virtually all aspects of the accounting, including deposits, checks, payroll, and reconciliations. The business was large enough to have a controller to whom she reported.

Each month the bookkeeper reconciled the bank accounts and maintained the bank statements along with the reconciliations in her files. At around the time of the fiscal year-end, the controller asked the bookkeeper to forward her reconciliation along with the bank statement, to be used for preparing financial statements and tax returns. The bookkeeper prepared a work-paper analysis of the reconciliation, listing the outstanding items, and reconciling the system balance to the bank balance. The controller was pleased to receive the requested information, which was used to satisfy the accountant's request for supporting schedules.

Based on the accountant's recommendations, the controller requested the following month's reconciliation from the bookkeeper. The controller knew she reconciled the bank statement through the system, and rather than preparing the work paper she had previously prepared, he asked for the actual printed reconciliation from the system. This was something he had never asked for in the past.

Week after week, excuse after excuse, the bookkeeper failed to deliver the printed bank reconciliation to the controller. After waiting long enough, the controller demanded that she go back and print the reconciliation and bring it to his office. She finally admitted that she had not completed the reconciliation as she had indicated and needed time to complete it. Furious, the controller assigned the reconciliation to another employee to complete. That employee identified issues relating to old uncleared transactions as well as the fact that the balance reported last month by the bookkeeper was significantly higher than the actual bank balance. In fact, the employee determined the account had not been reconciled through the system in close to two years.

The controller removed the bookkeeper, and the designated employee reconciled the account month by month for the two-year period. In the end it was determined the bookkeeper was skimming funds from the account and concealing her thefts by preparing manual work papers, forcing the reconciliations to balance. This was accomplished under the direct scrutiny of the controller, who could have simply asked for the system-generated reconciliations and bank statements at any month-end during the period.

The controller left the business prior to the completion of the investigation. The business lost close to $100,000 over the two-year period, and the bookkeeper was terminated and arrested. However, as with most embezzlers, she was determined to be insolvent and without any means for recovery, so further civil actions against her to recover the diverted funds were declined. In addition, the business needed to hire two new employees, a costly undertaking to the business owner in and of itself, along with the interruptions encountered while the positions were vacant.

Case Study 11.4 shows what can happen if you simply receive a reconciliation without the corresponding bank statement and system report reflecting the balance and activity per your system.

■ ■ ■

Reviewing bank statements, monitoring inventory and supplies, signing every check, verifying payroll, and reconciling deposits are all excellent controls and measures to be performed in some cases daily throughout each month. However, due to the creative nature of fraud, these measures still may not be sufficient to prevent or detect an employee theft or embezzlement.

In the next chapter our attention turns toward measures to be performed at the end of each month. Financial statements and reports need to be generated and reviewed every month to allow you to identify any unexplained activity that occurred during the month.

Bank Statements, Canceled Checks, and Reconciliations: Considerations

Bank Statements/Investment Statements	Completed
Receive the monthly statements directly and unopened.	❏
Consider having the bank statements mailed directly to your residence.	❏
Review the monthly statements for reasonableness, including deposits, electronic deposits, checks, withdrawals, electronic withdrawals, debit card activity, and ATM withdrawal transactions.	❏
Initial the monthly statements once your review is completed, and forward them to a designated employee for reconciling.	❏

Canceled Checks

Review your bank statements to determine if you receive your checks, images, or access online.	❏
Visit your bank and determine what other options are available to you to get your canceled checks or images of the fronts and backs for your review.	❏
Once you have gained access to your canceled checks or images, review them for reasonableness each month.	❏

(continued)

187

(Continued)
Bank Reconciliations

Ensure that bank reconciliations are being completed and printed each and every month. ❑

Ensure that the completed reconciliations are being attached to the supporting bank statements and being forwarded to you for review. ❑

Ensure that stale-dated outstanding items are being addressed in a timely fashion and not simply carried on the lists month after month. ❑

Initial the completed reconciliations and return them attached to the supporting bank statements to the designated individual for filing. ❑

CHAPTER 12

Financial Reports

I have had the pleasure of meeting many small business own- ers throughout my professional career. Builders, store owners, restaurant and bar proprietors, physicians, dentists, landscapers, florists, bookkeepers, beekeepers, cabinet makers, machinists, musicians, engineers, and mechanics ... to name a few. Each owner had something in common with the others, regardless of the industry. Every owner was extremely knowledgeable in his or her field, which allowed them to develop and oper- ate successful businesses and create job opportunities for their employees.

Unfortunately, there was another common trait among far too many owners: They lacked the financial sophistication to track and measure the financial performance of their business, or they didn't allocate sufficient time in their schedules to do so. Many viewed the financial area as more of a bookkeeping chore and happily delegated the related responsibilities (making deposits, writing checks, and paying employees) to an employee or outside consultant. As long as there were sufficient cash bal- ances in the bank and bills were being paid, they assumed that things must be operating properly. With luck the individual in charge of their finances proved to be honest and diligent in fulfilling his or her job responsibilities, but if that were true every time, I wouldn't have any case studies or stories, and there would be no need for a book on how small business owners can protect themselves from employee theft and embezzlement.

Generate Financial Reports Regularly

Using the back-to-basics approach, traditional bookkeeping for small businesses included processing the accounting information at the end of each month, closing the books for the month (which really meant no further transactions or activity could be posted to the closed month), and generating financial reports to be reviewed and maintained. Historically the month-end routine was standard month after month, and in many large companies, the month-end process hasn't changed. Publicly traded businesses continue today to process their month-end and produce financial results for each period, a requirement of being publicly traded.

However, small businesses seem to have migrated away from the month-end concept, with each month simply blending into the next. The day after a month-end has become simply the next business day in an ongoing 365-day period until the year-end. Many software packages originally designed with the month-end close concept have migrated to allow all months to remain open; no longer must one month be closed before activity can be posted to the subsequent month. Thus bookkeeping continues day after day until the end of a year, and in some cases with packages like QuickBooks, nothing special must be completed or processed at the end of a fiscal year. For those systems, one year simply transitions into the next, day after day, year after year.

If month-end processing is no longer required and performed, and if financial reports are no longer generated as part of that monthly process, at what point should the owner request financial reports to measure business performance? I suspect the answer depends on the needs and sophistication of the business owner.

Case Study 12.1   Is the Balance Sheet Supposed to Balance?

One recent project that stemmed from my involvement as a board member with a local nonprofit organization required me to assess the current capabilities of the business manager. Month after month I worked with two other accountants on the board to determine the financial reports and implement controls and procedures to address financial concerns with and beyond the financial reporting. Month after month the financial reports continued to be inaccurate and unreliable. Although it was a small organization with a paid individual responsible for the bookkeeping, the situation didn't improve.

Finally after discussing the matter in executive session, a determination was made to terminate the business manager, and the plan was executed immediately. The problem was that the replacement had not been identified, and since I was the catalyst behind the move, I was appointed interim business manager until a permanent replacement was hired.

After filling that role for nearly a year, I had implemented the proper controls and procedures required of the accounting areas and developed reliable financial reports that were distributed and reviewed monthly with the board's finance committee. This unprecedented information exchange and new meeting schedule changed the future of the organization.

(continued)

(Continued)

Unfortunately, the organization hired a new executive director who came in with his own ideas and opinions, and quickly alienated all those who had devoted so much of their time and effort to turn the organization around. As part of the transition, the new leader hired his own business manager, and my role finally ended. I left message after message for the new business manager to meet and transition what I had done, but I received no return calls. Rather, I was directed to provide all the accounting files and records to the business office, and the new individual would handle matters going forward. As my role ended as business manager, so did my term on the board. I stayed active with the organization but not in any official capacity.

Over the next two years I watched as the financial situation deteriorated, and all the controls, procedures, and reporting I helped to implement were eroded. Two years went by with no financial reporting or oversight, and eventually the new board was back in a position similar to the one we were in several years earlier, except that the organization's funds had disappeared.

A new director was finally hired, bringing along yet another new business manager. The old business manager who had eroded the reliability of the bookkeeping was paid to leave (after threatening to sue the organization), and the resulting books and records (a real mess) were left for the next person. The organization never fully determined what happened in that two-year period, as many of the accounting records could not be located. The results of that two-year period were hundreds of thousands of dollars in costs, potentially uncollected (or diverted) income, serious overspending, unexplained differences, and reductions in account balances. Even with the new individuals in place and a new board, the organization may not recover from the damage caused by the two individuals.

Where was the board while this happened? Well, I knew many of the board members, and I asked them similar questions throughout the two-year period. I was told that when they met, which was no longer monthly as I had established, the business manager was never present. Although the financial reports were requested time and again, they were never provided. Rather, the director strong-armed the board members around the financial issues and prevented them from ever seeing information or getting access to determine what was happening.

I tell all business owners I meet with that regardless of whether their systems require a month-end closing, they should impose a month-end process to ensure that certain things happen every month, just as they used to when owners were forced to close the books each month. The imposed monthly process would include ensuring that bank accounts are reconciled, cash receipts for the month are reconciled, payroll costs are reconciled, and any significant balances are reviewed and reconciled each and every month. For some small businesses, the bank reconciliations, cash receipts, and payroll could be the extent of the monthly processes.

Once completed, certain financial reports should be generated and provided to the owner for review. The same reports should be printed and maintained within a binder, categorized by month, to be available as needed to analyze the business's performance, regardless of the fact that the same reports could be reproduced from the system at any given time in the future. In almost every system, certain reports are date sensitive; if they are not run regularly and maintained each month, those reports cannot be regenerated at some future time. Accounts receivable and accounts payable reports tend to fall into this category, as do certain inventory reports.

Unless the business operates on a completely manual book-keeping system, most accounting packages include some level of financial reporting. Common packages like QuickBooks provide extensive reporting, better than most packages that cost significantly more to purchase and operate.

A list of the minimum reports you should generate or have generated for your review at the end of each and every month is presented here.

- **Balance sheet:** Lists your assets (i.e., cash balances and accounts receivable), accounts payable, and any other liabilities
- **Income statement:** Lists your income and expenses
- **General ledger:** Identifies every transaction within every account for the month
- **Accounts receivable detail:** Lists all customers with outstanding balances due, detailed by transaction
- **Accounts payable detail:** Lists all the vendors with outstanding invoices you owe them, detailed by invoice
- **Inventory detail:** Lists all inventory on hand, if applicable

The balance sheet and income statement reports can be run to include additional information, such as prior-period balances (i.e., balance sheet this month and the same month last year, and income statement for this month, year-to-date, and the same month and year-to-date for the previous year).

Once generated, the monthly financial reports should be forwarded to you for your review. For any balances that appear unusual, you should use the detailed general ledger report to review the transactions that comprise the account balance for the month. If issues are unresolved based on the transactions, you should talk with the designated employee who maintains the accounting for your business to resolve your questions. You could also share the financial reports with your outside accountant to address any unresolved issues.

Ideally you should set up a three-ring binder with 12 monthly tabs and maintain the monthly reports in the binder after completing your review. This system will allow you to review past months' reports while reviewing current performance, results, and balances, without the need to locate prior financial reports in a file or drawer or have them regenerated from the system.

Why Is the Regular Review of Financial Reports So Important?

Depending on the nature of an employee theft or embezzlement scheme, the cost associated with the diverted funds will ultimately be reported on your financial reports. Some schemes will be included directly in the results and balances, such as a disbursement scheme where an employee is paying unauthorized bills through the business's accounts. The amounts of each unauthorized check will be reported within one of the account balances during the period, likely within an expense account's activity. The same holds true for any payroll schemes, where an employee diverts funds from the business through unauthorized or fictitious payroll transactions. The costs associated with the payroll scheme will be included within the affected account's activity and balances, likely causing a higher-than-expected balance or result in those accounts.

For other schemes, the costs will still be reflected within the reports but not directly in a certain account. This is the case of a cash skim, where sales proceeds are diverted and not reported (or deposited) to the business. The skimmed sales will not be included within the business's sales and deposit amounts for the period, but the cost of the fraudulent activity for the period will appear as a decrease in the activity and balances due to the diverted sales.

In order to look at the balances within the accounts at the end of each period, review the financial results for the period, study the trends in balances and performance, and compare expected results against actual results, you need to generate and review the financial reports monthly, looking for differences, unexplained activity, or unexpected balances. A review of your cash balances compared to sales and accounts receivable should show whether you have collected on those sales, who still owes your company money, and how old the outstanding invoices are, as well as identify whether employees are diligently performing their invoicing and collections jobs. Your review of the cash balances compared to accounts payable will show you if you have sufficient cash to satisfy your obligations to vendors and employees as well as identify if vendors are not being paid on a regular basis (this may be evidence of frequent insufficient cash to pay vendors during times when sales are strong—a potential red flag).

Overall, your regular review of the financial reports can provide you with the earliest clue about a potential problem in your business.

When to Consider Outside Advice and Assistance

Most small business owners establish a relationship with an outside accountant to provide, at minimum, required tax compliance services, such as preparing annual tax returns for the business. Owners meet with their accountant annually to provide the minimal records required to file the tax returns and receive no prospective advice regarding the financial health of the business. Some owners maintain a significant relationship with their accountant and rely extensively on that person to oversee their business financially, reconcile accounts and balances, give advice on how to better operate the business, and provide tax savings strategies before the fiscal year ends. Regardless of the level of interaction, the important thing is that a business owner has a relationship with a qualified accountant. The owner can then choose how much or how little of the accountant's services are desired or needed, largely dependent on the sophistication of the business, how financially savvy the owner is, the accounting systems used to financially track the business, the level of internal capacity in the business created through employees, and, likely most important to the owner, the costs associated with the services.

A second set of eyes on your financial reports and regular detailed journals by your outside accountant provide another opportunity to identify potential issues and trends that warrant further analysis and investigating.

For small businesses with few employees and limited bookkeeping capabilities, using an outside bookkeeping service or an accountant to manage the books and records, reconcile your bank accounts, and provide financial reports may be appropriate, as there may be no other means to accomplish these critical functions. For businesses with in-house bookkeeping and an accounting system, the recording, reconciling, and reporting should be accomplished within the company rather than incurring outside fees. A better use of business funds could be to have your outside accountant evaluate the financial results and balances, as well as the financial health of the business, on a periodic basis. A quarterly review could help ensure that employees are completing the reconciliations as required and could provide sufficient insight into the company's performance to provide business and tax strategy advice to better manage the business. I am a big advocate of paying professional fees for advice rather than paying for processing, especially if there is processing capacity within the company.

Case Study 12.2   Oh, Let Me Fix That so the Amounts Agree

A colleague was brought in by a bank to perform an independent and objective review of the accounting records of one of the bank's customers as part of their loan agreement. Having outside accountants review customer businesses on the bank's behalf is not uncommon. If more of these reviews were performed on a more frequent basis, perhaps the banks would not suffer the losses to financial fraud that they currently face.

The customer's business was solely owned and relatively small in size, with one bookkeeper to complete most of the accounting needs for the company. The bookkeeper had been with the company for many, many years and was so trusted that the owner had her complete his personal bank accounts as well.

While reviewing transactions, including purchases and paid invoices, the auditor identified that manual checks were written to pay all company bills, a surprise in this day and age with computers and system-generated checks. The auditor selected a sample of transactions to review, including the original bank statements for two months during the period under review. While flipping through the checks, the auditor identified a check that didn't seem to make sense. The dollar amount in the box did not agree with the written dollar amount on the check. The check was a reimbursement check to the bookkeeper for purchasing bagels and other sundries for meetings, and the check was only for $1,200 (not a very big check for this business). Without alerting anyone, the auditor traced the check to the manual ledgers and noticed that the amount on the ledger agreed with the written amount.

Puzzled how this could occur with the carbon strip on the back of the checks that caused the entry on the ledger pages, the auditor asked the bookkeeper how the difference could occur. The bookkeeper looked at the check, took out a pen, and updated the amount in the box on the canceled check to match the written amount. Problem solved—the amounts now agreed.

The auditor thanked the bookkeeper for her help, then went back to the office and pulled every check payable to the bookkeeper in the two months of bank statements. The auditor then asked for all the monthly bank statements and canceled checks for every month during the two-year period. Flipping through the checks, the auditor located every check payable to the bookkeeper. As he looked at each check, he noted that the writing was slightly different on the amount written on the check itself, as if the written amount was entered or changed after the check was written (and likely signed).

The auditor went to discuss more of the checks with the bookkeeper, but she had left for the day and would not return until morning. Not wanting to wait until then, the auditor showed the checks to the owner, who proceeded to flip out. Each check written was over $1,000, and the owner said that every check should have been to reimburse the bookkeeper for less than $200. The owner substantiated the auditor's theory that the check amount had been changed after he signed the checks. For the one check initially identified by the auditor, the bookkeeper clearly messed up by not updating the amount in the box (except when it was updated for the auditor).

The owner was waiting with the auditor when the bookkeeper arrived for work the next morning. Confronted

(continued)

(Continued)

with the information, the bookkeeper insisted on meeting with the auditor alone, which the owner allowed. She stated that the owner was the individual changing the checks. She explained that the owner would send employees to the bank to cash the check and bring back the cash to the owner for his personal use.

The auditor returned to meet with the owner separately. Upon hearing what the bookkeeper had said, he confronted the bookkeeper, demanding to know why she had made up the story and threatening to have her arrested. The word "arrested" appeared to be magic; the bookkeeper then broke down and confessed to the scheme. She admitted that she had been altering signed checks for years.

Had the bank not sent in outside auditors to review the business records on its behalf, I wonder if the owner would have ever learned of his bookkeeper's scheme.

Receiving your annual information as part of the tax return preparation will provide little to no opportunity for your accountant to detect potential signs of employee theft or embezzlement within your company. Often the limited information provided lacks the transactional details needed to detect a potential problem.

The second set of eyes on your financial reports and detailed journals by your outside accountant provide another opportunity to identify potential issues and trends that warrant further analysis and investigating.

■ ■ ■

The final step in a monthly accounting cycle once the financial reports have been generated and reviewed is to assure yourself that the accounting system has been safeguarded. Although it would be best if the systems were secured and backed up daily, that may not be the case in many small businesses. Therefore, these measures should be incorporated into the month-end process to ensure that they are completed at least monthly. Detailed discussions of how to secure and safeguard your bookkeeping and accounting systems are presented in the next chapter.

Financial Reports: Considerations

Month-End Processing   **Completed**

Determine if your business completes a ❑
month-end close or month-end processing.

Implement month-end processing routines as ❑
needed to ensure that all activity has been
recorded, accounts have been reconciled,
and reports have been generated.

Financial Reporting

Identify the standard list of financial reports ❑
that need to be generated at the end of
each month.

Ensure that the standard financial reports are ❑
generated at the end of every month.

Review and maintain the standard financial ❑
reports each month, identify any unusual
or unexpected results or balances, and
investigate any identified items.

Ensure that your financial staff establishes ❑
and maintains a financial reporting
binder containing the monthly financial
reports.

Outside Accountants

Determine the extent and frequency of ❑
services to be provided by your outside
accountant.

Provide your accountant with copies of the financial reports. ❏

Solicit feedback and advice from your accountant regarding the finances of the business. ❏

Consider meeting with your accountant to review results and recommendations. ❏

CHAPTER 13

Safeguarding Your Bookkeeping or Accounting Systems

Although computers exist in most small businesses today, some business owners continue to maintain their accounting records manually. This chapter presents a brief discussion on how those owners should safeguard their manual checkbooks, ledgers, and other bookkeeping records.

The chapter also discusses how business owners who maintain their bookkeeping and accounting on a software system can safeguard software applications and company files. Depending on the size and nature of your business, you may have one program or several. Also, to further complicate things, your systems may be integrated, or one program may not be connected (talk to or share transactions) with your other systems. For example, a medical or dental office likely maintains a robust system to schedule patients, store medical information, process charges, record payments, and track outstanding balances. The same practice likely also utilizes a separate accounting system like QuickBooks to track bank deposits, write checks, record payroll costs, and produce financial reports. I have yet to see the two systems electronically connected (integrated). Similar system issues exist for other businesses, such as a bowling alley, movie theater, or restaurant (usually the smaller ones), to name a few, where the point-of-sale system (used to record sales to customers) is not typically integrated to the accounting system.

One particular accounting package, QuickBooks, seems to be utilized by more small businesses than any other package. The attributes of QuickBooks, like its ease of use, flexible reporting, and relatively low cost, are probably why it is so commonly used today. However, in my opinion, QuickBooks is also the system that is most susceptible to manipulation. When it is not configured and monitored properly, it creates a huge risk to a small business owner. Therefore, a separate discussion devoted strictly to the use of QuickBooks is included.

Manual Bookkeeping Systems

Limiting unauthorized access and safeguarding your bookkeeping records under a manual system should be very straightforward. All checkbooks and blank check stock, as well as the bank statements and the canceled checks (or images), should be maintained in a locked drawer or cabinet with access limited to authorized individuals. If you have a designated office within your business, safeguarding these records could include a locking file cabinet within your locked private office, providing a double level of security. Some small business owners simply maintain the accounting records at their homes, altogether removing any employee access to these records. On days when checks are needed, the owner simply brings the checkbook and checks into the business, and takes them home at the end of the day. More common, though, is an owner who simply writes and mails out checks directly from his or her home.

Payroll records also need to be secured and locked, limiting access to authorized individuals. Payroll records include the employee personnel files inclusive of payroll tax election forms such as Internal Revenue Service Form W-4, state withholding form (if applicable), Form I-9, and any other employment-related forms as well as the weekly or biweekly payroll registers, reports, and compensation information. As with the manual checkbooks, many small business owners choose not to maintain the payroll records on business premises and simply maintain these records at their home.

Regarding sales and customer payments, how these records are safeguarded largely depends on the nature of the business.

Case Study 13.1   When Generic Is Not Fashionable

A local hardware store I frequent maintains a stand-alone cash register at the front of the store. I have never seen any other cash registers, and the receipt I receive whenever I purchase something there is generic (name of store, date, items listed by cost only, subtotal, tax, and total). The register is of the type that I could purchase at my warehouse club and isn't connected to any larger, behind-the-scenes sales or accounting system. Every time I shop there I watch and note just how easy it would be for me if I were a dishonest employee wanting to steal from the business. Whenever I have returned an unwanted item, the same employees processed my return as had recorded my original sale. There is a key slot available for a second key to process returns and voids, but the store's owner simply leaves that key in the register at all times. It makes no sense to me. A dishonest employee could simply ring fictitious returns every day and divert funds from the register, with little or no risk of being caught. If you have one of these cash registers, my advice is to keep the second key out of the register and with you or with someone you designate, only to be inserted and used to process returns or voided sales when needed.

For retailers with cash registers, the registers should be configured so that the cashiers cannot close them out during or after their shifts; rather, the manager or owner must use a special password or key to close out the registers.

In more sophisticated retailers, the registers are likely integrated with the sales system, capturing the transactions and activity of each register within a central system.

Nonretailers may simply use manual sales order forms to record their sales or record sales only as customer payments are received. Regardless of how sales and/or customer payments are tracked and received, if a form is used to record these transactions, I recommend the forms be prenumbered and that the numbered forms be tracked and reconciled.

Case Study 13.2   Lunch Is on Us (the Taxpayers)

I was eating lunch with a colleague at a diner earlier this year. There were two waitresses working, and the place included 10 to 12 tables along with a counter and several stools. The waitress took our order on a pad (known as a dupe pad) and brought it to a window to the kitchen, where someone took the slip to prepare our order. Within a few minutes the waitress brought us our lunches and left the written slip on the table. When we finished eating, I brought the numbered slip to the register (another manual cash register similar to the one at the hardware store) and watched as the waitress used a calculator next to the register to calculate what I owed. I handed her a bill larger than needed, and she counted back my change. Then I watched her put my numbered slip on the top of a pile of slips on the counter. As far as I could tell, my lunch order was never rung through the register. At the end of the shift, the register tape would likely have been printed to reconcile the drawer. My order would not have been included on the register tape, and the sales proceeds would not have been included in the drawer. I figure this practice creates two issues for the diner.

1. The owner may have directed employees to record sales orders in this fashion. If so, the likely explanation is that the owner didn't want to record all sales on the register tapes (likely for "tax planning" purposes). The numbered sales tickets would not be tracked or retained if that were the case; they simply would be discarded.
2. A dishonest employee could simply be skimming sales from the business by not recording sales orders and diverting the payments.

Either way, this order slip system will likely lead to problems for the business owner. However, if a dishonest employee was skimming, and if the owner tracked the prenumbered sales tickets to be reconciled to the register tape, the skim would likely be detected (if it hadn't been deterred in the first place).

In conclusion, if you keep your bookkeeping manually, lock up your business records and limit access to them. If you use any forms in your business to track purchases, sales, or any other activity, consider numbering the forms and tracking the numbering sequences, looking for any gaps.

Computerized Bookkeeping and Accounting Systems

Even if your business utilizes a software package for bookkeeping and accounting purposes, my recommendation on tracking the forms used still applies. Any forms used in conjunction with your system, such as blank check stock, purchase orders, sales invoices, employee expense forms, and time cards, to name a few possibilities, need to be tracked. Consider requiring all the forms you use to be prenumbered. As with your checks, track the numbering sequences of your forms to ensure that no gaps exist in sequencing, which would alert you to a potential problem. Keep all your blank forms and financial information locked up when not in use, with access limited to authorized individuals. It is not uncommon for small businesses to leave unprinted check stock in a second tray of the laser printer for ease of processing. With this practice, think about who has access to your check stock sitting in the printer. The answer is everyone who comes near the printer, including any cleaning staff who come in during after hours when the business is closed.

Regarding the computer systems themselves, there are three primary risks that every small business owner should address:

1. Who has access to the systems, and in what capacity?
2. How are the files safeguarded and preserved?
3. How can your proprietary information be protected from theft?

Although I have a pretty extensive computer background working with small businesses in implementing both hardware and software solutions, I intentionally keep my experience quiet to allow business owners, employees, and outside consultants to explain their systems and their rationale behind the system decisions they have made. In some cases I have agreed with their selection, configurations, and policies; in other cases I have challenged their rationale. Only in those situations do individuals learn of my background, which often surprises them.

Regardless of what systems are implemented and who is responsible for them, I frequently ask small business owners 10 questions about their systems:

1. Who has overall access to your systems?
2. Who has specific access to the bookkeeping or accounting systems?
3. How is access controlled, and who manages who has access?
4. Do any of your systems allow users to change or delete transactions or activity?
5. How do you monitor user access to, and activity of, your systems?
6. Can anyone outside of the business premises access the systems?
7. How do you monitor outside access to ensure that only authorized individuals have accessed your systems?
8. Where do the system and company files reside?
9. How are the system and company files backed up and secured in the event of a disaster?
10. How would you know if an employee copied your proprietary information (e.g., your customer or client list, employee list, product list and sales information, and other company-specific information)?

Who Has Overall Access to Your Systems?

Access to your systems, whether you have a single computer or a network, should be limited to you (and any other owners) and those designated individuals who require access to the systems. Each individual should have a unique user ID and password assigned, and each user should be required to change the password on a periodic basis. You should also have a policy prohibiting employees from sharing user IDs and passwords and a second policy requiring employees to log out or freeze their screens with passwords whenever they are logged in but away from their work area. Each user should have access and rights to only those areas within the systems that correspond to his or her responsibilities. User IDs, e-mail accounts, and any other access information should be frozen or deleted as soon as an employee is terminated from employment, regardless of why the individual no longer works for your business.

Who Has Specific Access to the Bookkeeping or Accounting System?

Access to your bookkeeping and accounting systems should also be limited to you (and any other owners) and those few individuals who work in this area of the business. Just as with the access to the computers themselves, each authorized individual should have a unique user ID and password assigned to access the application, and each user should be required to change the password on a periodic basis. Within the bookkeeping or accounting system, each user should have access and rights to only the areas within the programs that correspond to his or her financial responsibilities.

How Is Access Controlled, and Who Manages Who Has Access?

You (the owner) should maintain a user ID and password established with the highest level of capabilities of the system, often referred to as the administrator-level user, or "admin" user. You should not share this user account with anyone, not even with outside information technology (IT) support solutions. Rather, create separate user IDs established with the administrator equivalent for those who require that level of system access, but remain in control over all user IDs by restricting the use of the admin user.

You or someone you designate should monitor user activity within the systems. This delegated, authorized user should use his or her assigned user ID, not your admin user ID. In the event a user forgets a password or similar problem, you or your designated administrator-level user can simply reset the user's password.

Do Any of Your Systems Allow Users to Change or Delete Transactions or Activity?

Users should have the ability to enter transactions and information into your systems based on their job responsibilities. Authorized users should have the ability to modify or change transactions as needed, as long as the systems include the capabilities to produce an audit report showing all the modifications and changes posted by all users during a defined period. *No users* should have the ability to delete posted transactions or information from your systems. Voiding original transactions due to an entry error or required change would be acceptable, but the original transactions should never be deleted. If your systems allow for users to delete posted activity or transactions, and the system cannot be configured to disable this feature, you will need to identify and produce a report each month detailing every deleted transaction for your review and scrutiny. Prevent what you can, and detect what you cannot prevent.

How Do You Monitor User Access to, and Activity of, Your Systems?

Many systems create an audit log or audit report that allows an owner or designated user to monitor user activity within the system. In some cases the audit report shows all activity for a period; in other cases the audit log simply shows exceptions, such as changed, modified, voided, or deleted transactions or activity. Regardless of what is reported by your system, the first thing to determine is whether your system has such audit reporting capabilities and, if so, whether they have been enabled (turned on). Some systems include the capabilities, but they are available only if the option is selected to enable the tracking. The tracking files can become voluminous, and therefore some people who install the systems keep the features turned off to preserve hard drive space. My advice: Turn the tracking features on, and establish a routine to review and purge the logs and reports to minimize the file sizes.

Presuming these capabilities are available and enabled, you (or someone you delegate) should be monitoring user activity by running the audit reports on a regular (daily or monthly) basis and reviewing the activity for reasonableness. Investigate the underlying explanations for any unusual activity or trends. Employees should be made aware that the audit reports are being reviewed, as your review could deter potentially dishonest employees for fear of getting caught.

Third-party software solutions may also be available that are compatible with your bookkeeping or accounting system, allowing you to monitor user activity, if such capabilities do not exist directly within your system.

Can Anyone Outside of the Business Premises Access the Systems?

Most small business systems are self-contained within the premises. Even if networked with several workstations, cash registers, and servers, all of the computer hardware is typically housed within the business. Users must be physically present at the business to gain access to the systems and programs. This configuration is easy to manage from an unauthorized access perspective, as users who cannot gain physical access to your computers likely cannot gain access to the systems.

In some cases the systems are configured to allow access from beyond the business premises. The owner may need or want to access the systems from his or her residence, the outside IT support company may need to access the systems for monitoring and troubleshooting, and authorized employees may need to access the systems while at home or out in the field. Regardless of the reason for providing outside access to your systems, limit such access to as few individuals as possible. Although outside access is convenient, it creates risks to the business, making the systems vulnerable to the threat of potential unauthorized access by someone hacking through the outside connection. If no outside access exists, the risk of unauthorized access is minimized.

Any outside access must be controlled with a separate level of security, user IDs, and passwords. Ideally outside access should be restricted to identified computer addresses, and only users using computers with the identified addresses can access the business's systems. Firewalls, virus protection, and encryption should also be considered vital components in your protection from unauthorized access to your systems from outside your business premises.

How Do You Ensure that Only Authorized Individuals Have Accessed Your Systems?

Just as you should monitor users' activity within your systems, you should monitor who has accessed, or attempted to access, your systems from outside the business. Most configurations used to accomplish outside access include a means for monitoring who has accessed the systems as well as attempts by unauthorized individuals to gain access. It is important to know if someone is consistently trying to access your systems, as changes could be warranted to further prevent potential access breaches to your systems.

Where Do the System and Company Files Reside?

On a single computer system, the company's data files reside on the computer's hard drive. The hard drive is most often an internal hard drive, but with the external hard drives available today, the data could exist on either. I recommend that company files and data be maintained on the internal hard drive. If an external hard drive is available, it can be used to image or back up the primary hard drive.

If your business operates on a network, the systems and files could reside on a file server hard drive or locally on one of your computer's hard drives. Ideally the programs and data files should be maintained on the file server hard drive to enable central access controls and backup solutions, allowing authorized users and workstations to access the programs and files on the file server. It is not uncommon for most programs to be configured in that fashion, but other programs may be installed and run locally on one computer, such as with payroll programs. It is common for the payroll employee to have the payroll program installed locally on his or her computer's hard drive, along with the company's employee files.

If certain programs have to be installed and run locally, the company's backup solution should include copying the hard drives of computers running local programs and files, or another protocol is needed to ensure that the data files on the local hard drives are somehow backed up regularly. Otherwise, the business runs the risk of data loss and interruption in service should anything happen to the computer or hard drive running the program.

Programs, folders, and directories on the file server should be created and configured with security in mind, to restrict individual users' access to only those areas they need to perform their job responsibilities. For example, the directory maintaining personnel and payroll information should be available only to authorized individuals, such as the owners and designated individuals responsible for those areas. No other users should have access to those areas. The same would hold true for the areas in which the accounting files are maintained.

How Are the System and Company Files Backed Up and Secured in the Event of a Disaster?

As mentioned, it is critical that your systems be backed up or imaged on a regular basis, to allow for recovery in the event of a disaster. The solution should be a comprehensive and complete backup of all the systems and files; ideally it should be performed daily. Programs and files run locally should be included in the backup configuration.

You should have multiple tapes or drives incorporated in your backup solution, allowing one backup to be maintained off-site at all times. Ideally a backup should be made each day and taken off-site. The previous day's backup should be brought in and used, leaving the most recent backup off-site. Further, a permanent backup should be maintained monthly and not reused in the backup cycle, to allow for recovery back to the most recent month in the event something happens with the daily backups. The monthly archive is a great method for introducing new tapes or media for backups, as the media you use should never be more than 6 to 12 months old.

In order to ensure that the backups are performed accurately and will be reliable in the event they are ever needed, you should access a backup on a periodic basis and restore a file at random from the backup media. This is the only way you will know if the backup solution is working and will be reliable.

If you designate an individual to perform and maintain the backups of your systems, you should periodically take the tapes home in place of the designated individual. Conversely, you could allow the designated individual to control the daily back-ups, but you could permanently control the monthly archives. In the event the employee is terminated or leaves the business, he or she will not have control of all the backup media. Employees should not be allowed to create their own backup solutions for their programs and files, such as copying their files onto

USB flash drives. If warranted, you can disable the USB ports on employee computers to prevent unauthorized copying of information onto USB devices.

Case Study 13.3   It Should Have Been Reliable

One of my long-term clients was a small medical practice located in the suburbs. The practice was pretty sophisticated, and many of its systems were automated. The practice maintained a local area network (LAN) with a single file server to support the systems and users. Installed on the server was an internal tape drive that was configured to make a complete backup of the server hard drive on a daily basis.

To ensure that the backup was performed adequately each day, and to safeguard the practice's systems in the event of a disaster or hard drive crash, one individual was designated to be responsible for checking the backup tape each day, removing the most recent tape, and inserting the next tape in rotation for the day's backup to be performed in the middle of the night. The most recent tape accompanied the designated individual home every day to ensure that the tape was maintained outside of the practice (an excellent procedure).

Day after day for two years the designated individual fulfilled these responsibilities and switched the tapes, taking the most recent one off-site. The person would come in on his day off and during vacations. If for some reason there was no possible way for him to get to the office, such as if he were going out of state, then he would identify someone else to change the tapes in his absence.

One day the server was down, as were all the systems for the practice. Frantic, the designated individual contacted

---

our firm for support assistance. (Our firm often fulfilled this role for our clients to the extent we could.) The designated individual learned that the hard drive within the server had crashed and that a new drive could be brought out within hours. Not the best news for the practice, but it would manage for the few hours until the systems were back online. The designated individual assured us the most recent tape was on-site and available to be restored onto the new drive once installed.

The new drive was installed and operational within hours, and the operating system was installed enough to allow the backup system to be reinstalled. Once installed and configured, the tape was inserted to start the restore process.

That's when the next issue was identified. The backup system indicated that the tape was blank, even though the designated individual told us the backup had run successfully the previous night. We asked for the previous night's tape. The practice would lose a day, but it wouldn't be a complete loss. Then we discovered that tape too was blank. In the next hour we checked all 14 tapes in their rotation, and all were the same as the first tape: blank.

Resolving the client's issue was a nightmare, and forever changed my view on tape backups and procedures regarding backups. I now ask questions about the tape backup system, how often the tapes are verified, how often the files are restored from tapes, and how old the tapes are in rotation. In this practice's case, the system was configured properly, but the physical cable connecting the tape drive to the tape controller and the computer motherboard had somehow become partially disconnected, preventing any files being

(continued)

(Continued)

copied onto the tapes. A simple step could have prevented the entire issue—randomly selecting a file on any tape on any day and restoring the file back onto the hard drive. That step would have told the designated individual there were no files on the tapes to restore. I have seen this issue about a half-dozen times with clients, but thankfully this was the only client that suffered data loss.

How Would You Know If an Employee Copied Your Proprietary Information?

The theft of proprietary information (e.g. customer names, client list, product information, vendor details) and intellectual property has become a major issue with employers of all sizes. Often the true value in the business resides with its client or customer list, products, trade secrets information, and other information. All too often trusted employees are lured away by a competing business or, worse, start a competing business, and violate their fiduciary responsibility to you, their employer, by attempting to poach your clients, customers, and employees. With their knowledge of your business practices, pricing, and other strategic information, they can do significant damage to your business and, in some cases, put you out of business. While these actions warrant civil and often criminal actions, the damage to the business has already been done, and recovery is the issue.

Your systems should include the ability to monitor users who require access to proprietary information. Your monitoring system should alert you if a user copies a large block of information, such as the customer list, and your policies should state that all company information remains the property of the company. You should have a policy and procedures to monitor e-mail activity and be alerted when a user e-mails a large file to himself or herself outside of the business, or worse, to a competitor.

Case Study 13.4 ~~Blood~~ Money Is Thicker than ~~Water~~ Blood

A successful local family business experienced an embezzlement that permanently affected their family relationships. Two brothers ran the business, and their sister was responsible for all the financial aspects of the company. Unfortunately, the brothers did not implement any controls over the sister's actions, and it wasn't until after the family split and the sister was removed from the business that the brothers learned what she had been doing with the company's finances. Besides diverting several hundred thousand dollars from the business through a series of different schemes, she also brought the company's accounting system home with her on a USB drive. It was later learned that another relative of the sister worked for a competing company, and bids were lost to that competing business. It seems pretty evident that the sister was taking the bid and customer information home on her USB drive and sharing the information with her relative. In one instance the company submitted the lowest bid for a contract. The competing business had submitted a higher bid, but after learning of the lower bid, resubmitted an even lower bid, winning the contract. The brothers never recovered the funds lost through her diversion. The damage she did by breaching her fiduciary duty and stealing proprietary information could never be measured, as there was no way to determine just how long she had been stealing and leaking information to at least one competing business.

If warranted, it is possible to lock down your systems even further by disabling the USB ports on individual computers and limiting file sizes as attachments on e-mails, preventing users from simply copying the files onto readily available portable devices or e-mailing them.

QuickBooks Users

If your business utilizes the accounting system QuickBooks, you need to address specific risks to minimize opportunities within that system that create vulnerabilities to your business. QuickBooks is a very robust, cost-beneficial, and effective accounting system and is widely used by many small businesses. The ease of setup and use along with its flexible reporting makes it an appropriate system in many contexts. However, because early versions of QuickBooks still in use today lack certain controls, including limited safeguards to prevent employee abuse and allowing too much freedom with the accounting information, they earn my designation as the most vulnerable systems in existence. Users can post, change, void, and delete anything previously posted to the system, and the system could be made to report anything a user desires, creating issues of system reliability.

More recent versions of QuickBooks have addressed some of these security issues and also added the ability to track user activity within audit logs and reports. However, unless the individual who installed and configured your QuickBooks system was knowledgeable and security conscious during the installation, many of the included safeguards may not be enabled, leaving your system wide open to potential opportunities.

If you use QuickBooks within your business, I strongly recommend that you speak with your accountant or someone experienced and credentialed specifically in that program to ensure that the safety and security features available have been enabled and utilized to preserve the integrity of the accounting information. I further recommend that you review audit logs on a very regular basis, even if the security features and password levels have been enabled, to ensure that your system has not been used to conceal dishonest acts by even your most trusted employees.

■ ■ ■

Employee fraud requires three components to adequately address the risks as well as allow for recovery. The three components form a triangle. Prevention and detection, two elements of the anti-fraud triangle, are the best measures available to owners, but they will not be sufficient to allow a business to recover financially in the event of an employee theft or embezzlement. The third component of the anti-fraud triangle, insurance coverage, is usually the only means to recoup funds or assets diverted by a dishonest employee. Insurance coverage issues are discussed in Chapter 14.

Safeguarding Your Bookkeeping or Accounting Systems: Considerations

Manual Bookkeeping Systems	**Completed**
Secure all accounting and financial records including payroll information, and restrict access to authorized individuals.	❏
Consider using prenumbered forms.	❏
Track the numbering sequences of any prenumbered forms, looking for gaps in any sequences.	❏

Computerized Bookkeeping Systems	
Consider using prenumbered forms in conjunction with your systems.	❏
Track the numbering sequences of any prenumbered forms, looking for gaps in any sequences.	❏
Control and monitor user access to your overall computer systems.	❏
Control and monitor user access specific to your accounting or bookkeeping systems.	❏
Control who provides individual users with their access and rights within the systems.	❏
Limit outside access to your systems as much as possible.	❏
Control and monitor all user activity conducted through outside access, including unauthorized access attempts.	❏
Centrally install all programs.	❏

Require all files to be centrally stored for access and backup purposes. ❏

Limit access within the systems, folders, and directories based on individual user responsibilities and need of access. ❏

Ensure that a complete system backup is performed on a regular basis, ideally daily, and control storage and access to the backups. ❏

Ensure that the backup media (tapes or drives) are fresh and reliable, less than 6 to 12 months old. ❏

Periodically review backups and restore randomly selected files from the backup medium to the original drives to ensure that the backup system is operating properly and the backup medium is reliable. ❏

Include monthly archives of backup media (tapes or drives) and control access to the archived media. ❏

Control and monitor all company-proprietary information to prevent and detect potential diversion of the information by a dishonest employee. ❏

QuickBooks

Consult with your outside accountant (if qualified) or an outside consultant credentialed by QuickBooks. ❏

(continued)

(Continued)

Ensure that all safety and security features have ❑
been enabled and utilized to protect the
integrity of your financial information and
minimize opportunities for users of the
QuickBooks system to manipulate, change,
delete, or otherwise alter accounting
transactions and balances.

Monitor the audit logs and reports on a regular ❑
basis for any unauthorized or unusual
activity, and immediately investigate any
instances identified.

CHAPTER 14

Prevention, Detection, and Insurance

A s discussed throughout the book, the approach required to address risks for employee theft and embezzlement must include three elements: prevention, detection, *and insurance*. Through the design and implementation of practical internal controls and accounting procedures, certain risks can be addressed to minimize the potential for theft and embezzlement. However, not every possible risk and scheme can be prevented, even with the best of controls. Therefore, further measures must be designed and implemented to detect actual instances of thefts and embezzlement as early as possible. The longer a scheme continues, the larger the loss to the business.

Prevention and detection simply aren't sufficient to address the risks. In the event a theft is detected, often there is limited or no means of recovering the diverted funds. As discussed in Chapter 2, employees typically steal to solve some financial need in their lives, and so the diverted funds are usually gone. The primary assets that could be used to provide restitution to your business are often limited to their residence and their car. The individuals may rent as opposed to owning a home, and even if they own their home, it is often fully encumbered with debt, leaving no equity for recovery. The same holds true for their cars, although even if owned outright, a car will likely provide little in the way of recovery.

This is why having adequate insurance coverage for employee theft and embezzlement is critical to any business's approach to the risks associated with having employees. The insurance policy is often the source of recovery for the business up to the policy limit, which is why a business carrying a minimal amount of coverage will recover only a minimal amount. The good news is that the cost associated with obtaining and maintaining employee dishonesty coverage is relatively low compared to other types of coverage. The bad news is that based on my experience, most insurance agents don't discuss this coverage with their clients, and consequently the business owner is unaware of the lack of coverage or inadequacy of coverage until a claim is required to be filed for recovery, and by then it is too late.

The days of obtaining fidelity bonds for each employee who handles any financial aspects are in the past, mainly due to the cost and inconvenience of having to bond each employee. With turnover issues, having bonds updated can become a burden. Bonds still exist but are mainly found with employees who handle any retirement plan responsibilities, especially since it is a requirement of the Employee Retirement Income Security Act (ERISA).

The most common type of coverage found today is employee dishonesty, also known as employee crime or employee theft. The coverage is commonly found within the business commercial package, and it can be part of the main policy or a rider or separate endorsement to the policy. The coverage is very straightforward, and typically includes the maximum loss amount as well as a deductible. The coverage will cover the cost of the loss, as defined by the policy, and in some cases there may also be coverage toward the cost of investigating the loss.

Timing Is Everything

Most policies treat an embezzlement scheme as one event regardless of when it started, how long it occurred, how many times a theft occurred, and how many schemes were involved. The same policies look at the coverage amounts in place during the duration of the schemes to determine how much coverage is applicable. For example, if a business maintained $10,000 coverage for five years and then last year increased its coverage amount to $100,000, it does not mean the company is insured for up to $100,000 for an entire scheme period, nor will the policies allow a claim filed against each year's policies (stacking of claims). After increasing its coverage, the business detects an employee has been embezzling funds. The final analysis shows the individual stole $100,000 from the business over the past three years, with $20,000 in the first year, $30,000 in the second, and $50,000 in the most recent year. The business would not likely recover the full $100,000 even though it was insured up to that limit per the most recent policy. Rather, the business would likely recover $60,000, less its deductible, provided it could substantiate its claim. The $60,000 would be calculated in this way:

Year 1	$20,000 stolen	$10,000 policy limit	$10,000 recovery
Year 2	$30,000 stolen	$10,000 policy limit	$0 recovery
Year 3	$50,000 stolen	$100,000 policy limit	$50,000 recovery
			$60,000 recovery

The $60,000 aggregate falls below the $100,000 policy limit in place at the time the embezzlement was detected and the insurance company was provided notice of a claim, so the $60,000 would be the expected recovery. This is different from making claims against each year's policy (stacking claims) discussed earlier. Had the company not increased its coverage amount from $10,000 to $100,000, the most it would have recovered was $10,000, less the deductible.

This is why it is important to ensure that coverage exists within the policy and to assess the adequacy of the coverage as early as possible. The longer the increased policy limits are in place, the more coverage that will be available to recover diverted funds.

Adequacy of Coverage

The amount of coverage you should carry for employee dishonesty is subjective to each business. The minimum amount of coverage I recommend to any business is $100,000, but I do not represent that maintaining this minimum amount provides you an adequate level of insurance. In my experiences where I have found that coverage did exist, the amount was limited to $10,000 or less. For most businesses that suffered a loss at the hands of an employee, that level of insurance was grossly inadequate for any substantial recovery. Adequacy is something that should be discussed with your insurance agent, and the amount of coverage you deem adequate should be sufficient to recover stolen funds that could cause the business to close.

Responsibilities for a Claim

Coverage for employee dishonesty commonly includes a description of responsibilities for the insured in the event of a claim or potential claim. Here are the responsibilities often encountered:

- Provide timely notice of a potential claim.
- Obtain and file a signed and notarized affidavit for proof of loss with substantiating documentation.
- Notify the appropriate law enforcement agency (not included in every policy).

- Cooperate with the investigation of the claim.
- Cooperate with the insurance company seeking recovery of the paid claim.

Provide Timely Notice of a Potential Claim

The insurance company wants to know as early as possible if a claim could be made against the policy. The issue is: When does something become worthy of providing notice of a potential claim? If the criteria to provide notice were met every time a drawer was short or inventory was missing, insurance companies could be getting notice on a daily basis. My experience has been that once something has been discovered in a business, preliminary investigative procedures need to be performed to determine the nature and extent of the discovery. Through that process, the earliest moment it can be determined that a potential loss could have been incurred is the time notice needs to be made in a timely fashion. The preliminary investigative measures need to be performed in a timely manner, and the importance of those measures is to ensure that there are no bona fide explanations for the identified discovery.

I have always advocated that counsel be consulted to discuss a potential claim, when and how notice will be provided, and also who should provide the notice. I also advocate that notice be limited to the minimal amount of information required to maintain the integrity of the investigation. If the policy indicates notice of a potential claim is required, then the notice should be limited to the owner indicating to the insurance company that the potential for a claim exists. No details, no names, no dates, and no amounts—just notice that a claim could exist. These policies never require more than that, and providing too much detail in advance of full investigative measures could be speculative at best. Once again, I recommend that counsel handles providing notice, or at least drafts the notice to be sent over to the insurance company. I also recommend that you start a file and track everything related to the case, and obtain in writing a statement from the insurance company that notice was provided.

File a Proof of Loss (with Supporting Information)

Once notice has been provided, the next thing that typically happens is the business will receive a proof of loss, or affidavit, or both, to be completed and filed. A new claim will have been established along with a due date, commonly 90 days. Find the due date, document it, and make everyone aware of the due date. One way to potentially have the claim denied is to miss the due date. Extensions are nearly automatic if requested, allowing more time to complete the investigation and compile a complete and accurate claim. Request an extension of time to file in advance of the original due date, and get the extension documented in writing. Additional extensions of time are not uncommon, as fraud investigations can take many months to complete. The key here is to make sure the due date(s) are never missed.

Once the investigation is complete, the proof of loss is signed, witnessed, and filed. The filing of the loss claim starts the clock for the claim to be reviewed and paid.

Notify the Appropriate Law Enforcement Agency

Some policies require law enforcement to be notified, while other policies are silent in this regard. Be sure to read the policy to preserve a potential claim. In my experience, many insurance companies interpret "notify law enforcement" as "you have to have the person arrested." If the policy states that the individual determined to be responsible must be arrested in order to collect on a claim, then it is likely that you will have to have the individual arrested (if law enforcement and the prosecutor will accept the case and pursue an arrest). However, most policies do not state that language. The policies commonly state that the insured must notify law enforcement. Notifying law enforcement and having someone arrested are two entirely different requirements. Here is where the business's counsel should be reading and advising the business owner of his or her responsibilities and options to preserve the claim.

Case Study 14.1   Read What They Wrote, Not What They Meant

A local business fell victim to an embezzlement scheme perpetrated by one of its managers. Proceeds from sales were diverted rather than deposited into the bank, and records were altered to conceal the thefts. Once the scheme was detected, the manager was terminated, and an insurance claim was initiated. The manager was renting an apartment with no other known assets of any substance, so incurring professional fees to chase the manager for restitution in civil court made no sense. Because the manager had already demonstrated instability prior to the theft being detected, the organization decided not to pursue criminal charges initially for fear of how the manager might react toward the organization and its employees.

In reviewing the insurance policy, the organization had coverage up to $100,000, along with the standard claim requirements. However, the policy also indicated that the business would need to "notify" law enforcement should there be evidence that a law had been broken. In meeting with counsel for the organization, I indicated that "notify" is much different from "have the person arrested," and as such in order to file a claim we would need to provide evidence

(continued)

233

(Continued)

that the police were in fact "notified." Counsel agreed with my approach, especially since the organization didn't want the manager arrested.

I drafted my report identifying the procedures and findings, and I knew the report would be used as the basis for the insurance claim. Next I went to the local police station along with the controller and had an officer brought in to take an initial complaint. After brief introductions, I indicated to the officer that we sought nothing beyond the meeting except for a copy of the initial report. The organization was not seeking an investigation or any criminal charges but merely accomplishing a requirement of the insurance policy by notifying the police. Confused, the officer asked why no investigation or arrest was warranted. The controller provided the officer more details and reiterated that all we needed was a copy of the report to show the police were "notified."

A few days later the controller retrieved a copy of the report, and the insurance claim was filed. A month later the organization received a check for the claim amount, less the deductible. A few months later the organization heard that the manager was being pursued by the insurance company to recover the payment made to the organization. They too were likely to find there were no assets and no means of recovery beyond a wage garnishment, which would take close to forever to repay the claim.

Cooperate with the Investigation of the Claim

The claims department of the insurance company may have the in-house sophistication to review and approve the claim or, more likely, will send your claim out to a contractor, such as an accounting firm, for review on behalf of the insurance company.

Often the insured business must cooperate with whoever is reviewing the claim to decide if it will be paid. Records and explanations are often sought to substantiate the loss. If the proof of loss was filed adequately along with supporting evidence, schedules, and analyses, there may be no inquiries to the insured.

Cooperate with the Insurance Company Seeking Recovery of the Paid Claim

When the claim is paid, the process does not necessarily end. More likely the insurance company will begin a case against the individual responsible for the loss and attempt to recover payment from that person. Most policies require that the insured cooperate with the insurance company in its efforts to recoup its payout.

Disclaimer

The discussions regarding coverage and claim processing are not meant to provide insurance or legal advice, and should be used strictly as practical information to better understand these areas. The information was based on over 22 years of experience with this type of coverage and these types of claims. A prudent business owner should realize that nothing substitutes for the professional advice and interpretations offered by duly qualified insurance agents and attorneys.

■ ■ ■

Being fully briefed on how to deal with the risks of employee theft and embezzlement, the final chapter addresses what you should (and should not) do in the event you discover a potential or actual theft or embezzlement issue within your business.

Prevention, Detection, and Insurance: Considerations

Prevention/Detection	**Completed**
Design and implement policies, controls, and procedures to prevent common employee theft and embezzlement schemes from occurring.	❏
Design and implement policies, controls, and procedures to detect as early as possible any potential thefts or embezzlements that were not prevented and actually occurred.	❏

Employee Dishonesty Insurance Coverage

Ensure that your existing policies include coverage for employee dishonesty (employee theft/employee crime).	❏
Assess the adequacy of your employee dishonesty coverage.	❏
Monitor the adequacy assessment as your business grows or changes.	❏
Identify your responsibilities under the policy in the event of a potential claim.	❏

Dishonesty Claim Filing

Identify when a potential claim could exist.	❏
Discuss the potential claim with counsel.	❏
Determine if notice needs to be provided to ensure a claim.	❏
Provide notice (or have counsel provide notice), and obtain proof that notice was provided.	❏

Prepare and timely file a proof of loss or other required forms for the claim, along with supporting documentation. ❑

Identify whether law enforcement involvement is required to ensure the claim. ❑

Cooperate with the insurance company during the claim review process. ❑

Cooperate with the insurance company while they pursue recovering the paid amount from the responsible individuals. ❑

CHAPTER 15

Your Response to an Identified or Potential Issue

A Dreaded Day of Discovery

Every business owner should have a relationship with an attorney, an accountant, and an insurance agent. Notwithstanding the need for their input and involvement should the day arrive that you detect a potential or actual instance of employee theft or embezzlement, each of these professionals can prove invaluable in providing feedback and advice respectively on numerous business- and employee-related issues. Depending on the size and structure of the business, a fourth relationship with a banker would also prove strategic in managing the cash requirements of the business. While not critical to the successful growth and operations of every business, having these existing relationships will prove invaluable if you discover a potential problem, whether theft or fraud related or with some other aspect of the business.

The day every employer dreads, the day every owner hopes never to encounter, happens to occur in your business. Something has caught your attention, whether provided to you by another individual or found on your own, and it may be the first indication that an employee may have stolen or embezzled from your business. If you are like most owners I have met, you will have lots of feelings and emotions racing through your head, potentially a state of panic, and you will likely be extremely eager to know more about the activity and why it occurred. With some luck you will have someone available to you at the time of your discovery who will assist you through the early process of understanding what it is you just discovered—someone to talk with who will help you remain rational while you figure out the next steps to take.

The most important thing you can do is to act as you would normally, not raise any immediate attention to the issue, and not do anything spontaneous or in response to the potential finding. In my experience, the fastest way to ensure a potential lawsuit brought by an employee or former employee (even one being pursued for stealing from you) is to immediately react to the potential finding, terminate the employee on the spot (or, worse, confront and harass the employee), say things you cannot take back, and behave toward the individual in a manner that cannot be undone or reversed. These emotional spontaneous reactions can create many issues for you down the road, especially if it is later found that there was no theft or embezzlement, or that the individual had nothing to do with it.

The best thing you can do is consider what you just discovered, and call counsel to discuss how you should proceed. Most small businesses do not have in-house counsel or an internal audit department, but if either exists, they would be appropriate parties to contact as well. My advice is to act normally and not do anything differently, as any change in your behavior or patterns could alert a dishonest employee who has been stealing from you to destroy the evidence and "get out of Dodge." You need to determine how you should proceed to ensure the integrity of your employees as well as the integrity of your inquiry or investigation into the discovery. The best way to do that every time is to discuss the discovery with counsel. If the attorney you have a relationship with does not specialize or have experience in the areas of employment and employee embezzlement, you should ask for a referral to another attorney who would be more qualified. Having the most appropriate professionals assist you in the potential matter will directly impact its successful resolution.

Case Study 15.1   It Had to Be Her!

A local nonprofit organization contacted me regarding missing funds. I went directly to the organization that day and met with the executive director, and I listened to him tell me how bad the former accountant was and how she must have stolen all this money from the organization. He was clear that he wanted her to be arrested and disbarred as a CPA, and that he also wanted to be sure she never worked in accounting again. As with every case, I listened to his story and took notes, but I remained open-minded and asked him questions about the organization as well as the issues he had identified. Time and again throughout the meeting he continued to badmouth and disparage the former controller, someone who had worked at the organization for several years but left recently to pursue a different opportunity.

I cautioned the director to remain open-minded until a complete investigation was performed and that he should be very careful about his disparaging remarks until it was proven that the controller stole the funds. He was adamant that the controller stole the funds and left before she was caught. He wanted to contact the police and have them begin a criminal investigation into the controller, with the hopes that her new employer would find out about it.

This case, the one that forever reminds me of the importance of objectivity, came to an end once I completed my investigation and determined there were no funds missing.

(continued)

(Continued)

The organization historically relied on funding from endowment funds to support operating losses. Each year as far back as I could determine there were large transfers from the endowments into the operating account. However, in the last two years, the same two years that a new capital campaign was under way, there were no transfers from the endowment accounts. Further, the last two years were the worst years for the organization financially from an operating perspective, requiring what should have been larger-than-usual transfers to support operations. And yet there were no transfers.

Quite simply, the capital funds that should have been placed into a special account were used for operations, which is why there was no need for transfers from the endowments. In order to correct the low balances in the capital account, the transfers that should have been made from the endowment accounts were simply made into the capital account to restore the balance. Case closed.

Now let's rewind back to the initial meeting, with the ranting and raving of the director. Had he initiated a criminal case, or had the former controller learned of the disparaging remarks, she would have had a great case of defamation and potentially libel against the director and the organization.

Should you find yourself without a relationship with an attorney, all is not lost. You should call a friend or business colleague for a referral to a qualified attorney. I recommend getting the names of a few attorneys and calling each one to determine whom you feel most comfortable speaking and working with in resolving the discovery. You should also inquire about their experiences in these specific types of matters.

In addition to not changing your behavior and not reacting emotionally and spontaneously, here are a few more things you should *not* do without conferring with counsel:

- Do not immediately contact your insurance company. At the initial discovery, it is unknown if there will be a potential claim or not. Therefore, there is no obligation to provide notice, as you don't even know what the discovery is yet.
- Do not immediately contact the police, unless you discover that a crime was just committed involving the business, an employee, or an owner (such as a robbery, burglary, assault, etc.), where the police and other emergency responders are immediately required for the matter. In most cases of employee theft and embezzlement, there is no immediate need for law enforcement or emergency services.
- Do not start talking about the discovery to anyone, and keep the circle of trust as small as possible until you can learn more about the discovery.
- Do not access employee computers, search employee computer files and folders, review employee e-mails and Internet activity, and potentially alert the culpable individual as well as potentially damage or destroy key information.
- Do not access employees' physical areas, such as desks, cabinets, and other work areas, as such actions could alert the individual and lead to destruction of evidence (as well as potentially become an invasion-of-privacy issue should employees have an expectation of privacy).

Due Diligence on the Discovery

Take things one step at a time. First, determine if your discovery is credible. What does the discovery involve? Start to identify what kinds of things could be done to learn more about the discovery, especially while waiting for counsel to call you back.

Don't start doing any of the potential steps or measures, but simply start looking at where information could be obtained. Review any information you may already have in your possession that could shed light on the discovery. The best thing to do is speak with someone independent, objective, and rational (and clearly not potentially involved or related to the discovery). Likely that is almost always counsel.

Having said that, sometimes things happen. Through no fault of your own or your actions, an employee could be alerted or start acting differently, perhaps even acting out, and could seek you out to discuss the discovery with you (or worse, come to confess to you about doing something). If things turn for the worse before you have a chance to seek counsel's advice, you will need to react to the situation, especially if an employee is destroying evidence or deleting computer files. In these extreme and unusual cases, you will need to remain rational and in control, but you will need to immediately remove the individual from the premises for everyone's safety and the preservation of any potential evidence. The best practice is to have the employee immediately leave the premises without returning to his or her work area, and place the individual on paid administrative leave. Termination of employment can be done later. The key is to avoid making any rash decisions that could cause risk and potential litigation down the road. By removing the individual from the premises and placing him or her on paid leave, the person has not been terminated. Once the individual has left the premises, you have time to obtain the advice of counsel before proceeding. In the event the individual appears to be a safety threat to themselves or anyone else at the business, consider the immediate assistance of law enforcement.

Whether nothing has happened since your discovery, or you were one of the unlucky ones who had to remove an individual from the business, eventually you will connect with counsel. The initial connection will likely be by phone. Based on the discovery, it may be limited to the phone call or it may cause the attorney to come to the business for a meeting. Each case is different, and each discovery dictates the level of response required. I am a big fan of meeting in person, if time permits, to discuss the discovery and investigative options. It is important for you to remain open-minded, even when an explanation for the discovery appears obvious. I remind you, just as I remind students in my forensic accounting class, to remain objective and not operate with tunnel vision. Many cases I have investigated that seemed to be obvious turned out to be something completely different than expected. Those are the cases I remember the most. Remember, employees are hard to replace, especially trained ones who have been loyal and dedicated to the business for many years. The last thing the business should want is to lose a key employee who was otherwise not involved, if something did in fact happen, due to how the employee was treated by his or her employer. Once a bond has been broken or trust has been violated, whether by an employee stealing or by an employer accusing an employee (or acting accusatory toward an employee), the relationship is often beyond repair.

Once counsel is on board, the next steps will be dictated by the facts and circumstances of the discovery. A second planning meeting could be warranted with the involvement of other professionals. Concerns for safeguarding records, paper and electronic, may be important before proceeding with procedures that could alert employees of your knowledge. This may require hiring professionals to image computer hard drives and preserve records, commonly completed after work hours unbeknownst to employees. Steps and measures can be implemented to identify more information about the discovery. The procedures may require the outside assistance of forensic accountants experienced in matters similar to the discovery. It is not uncommon for forensic accountants and forensic computer specialists to work closely to safeguard potential evidence to be used to further understand the discovery, as forensic computer special-ists can often find information and evidence to support a forensic accountant's investigation.

The main goal in working with advice of counsel should be for you to learn as much as possible about the discovery to deter-mine if legitimate explanations exist, or if you are dealing with a potential or actual occurrence of employee theft or embez-zlement. Once you have sufficient information to make that determination, subsequent courses of action can be identified and executed. In the event legitimate explanations are found, changes in controls, policies, and procedures may be warranted to prevent future occurrences of similar activity.

What If It Appears to Be Fraud?

In the event the explanations are fraud related, the best courses of action need to be discussed, taking into account your desired outcome of an investigation. Some of the considerations you will need to discuss with counsel and other professionals assisting are listed next.

- Does the potential for an employee dishonesty insurance claim exist, and if so, should notice of a potential claim be provided (and by whom)?
- What do you (the owner) seek as the outcome of the inves-tigative procedures (arrest, restitution, apology, etc.)?
- Is criminal prosecution desired, or will it potentially be required either by the insurance policy or for leverage to resolve the matter? If so, should law enforcement get involved with the matter?
- Does the potentially responsible party have any means of restitution, and should a civil case be initiated against him or her (if sufficient information is known)?

- Do sufficient records and files exist to complete contemplated procedures to reasonably determine who was involved, how much was involved, and the full details of the scheme?
- Do the estimated costs to complete the procedures appear reasonable to you in comparison to the potential amount involved in the matter (avoiding your spending good money after bad)?
- Do you have the means to pay for the professional fees?

With counsel and other professionals to assist you with these and any other potential issues in resolving the matter, you will need to proceed based on the advice you receive. No two cases are ever handled exactly the same way, as the fact patterns of every case are different. For this reason, there is no point in discussing investigative strategies and procedures further in this book. What could be written for one situation likely would not be applicable to any other situation.

I end this chapter similarly to how I have ended many meetings with potential victims of financial crimes, by wishing you the best of luck in favorably resolving your matter.

■ ■ ■

I hope you have found this guide helpful in educating yourself regarding how to establish proactive controls and procedures as well as in providing you a practical reactive roadmap to follow should a potential or actual theft or embezzlement issue arise within your business.

You should use the discussions in this book as a starting point and consider having your business evaluated by a qualified accountant or other specialist once you have implemented the recommendations in this book. Additional and more specific controls and procedures could be warranted based on your specific situation.

Appendix A provides you with insight from Lester Amos Pratt, a pioneer and leading expert in the field of internal controls geared toward preventing and detecting employee theft and embezzlement. I trust you will find them as insightful and relevant to today's business environments as they were when Mr. Pratt first wrote about them in his book published in 1952. More on Mr. Pratt's life and accomplishments follows in Appendix B.

Your Response to an Identified or Potential Issue: Considerations

Proactive Measures	Completed
Establish a relationship with an attorney for your business.	❏
Establish a relationship with an accountant for your business.	❏
Establish a relationship with an insurance agent for your business.	❏
Establish a relationship with a banker for your business.	❏

Reactive Measures

If something is detected, remain calm and rational, as normal as possible.	❏
Do not react emotionally, spontaneously, or reactively, as you cannot reverse your actions, and they could cause additional risks to the business.	❏
Contact counsel to discuss the issues and your options.	❏
Review your insurance policy, but wait to contact the company until after speaking with counsel.	❏
Discuss with counsel whether the police should be contacted. Generally there is time at a later date to get law enforcement involved.	❏
Limit whom you discuss the issues with, and keep the group as small as possible.	❏
Discuss with counsel when and how to conduct an investigation into the issues.	❏

(continued)

(Continued)

Consider how to preserve evidence without ❏
alerting employees.

Review your company's policies and ❏
procedures regarding locking workspace
areas, and determine if there is a potential
expectation of privacy.

Consider placing potentially responsible ❏
employees on paid administrative leave.

Consider the need to engage a computer ❏
forensic specialist to preserve electronic
evidence, such as imaging hard
drives.

Consider the need to engage a forensic ❏
accountant to conduct the investigation into
the issues.

Findings

If no theft or embezzlement is identified based ❏
on the investigation, consider identifying and
implementing changes to your controls and
procedures to prevent the activity from
occurring in the future.

If a theft or embezzlement is identified:

1. Notify the insurance company to preserve a ❏
claim against the policy in the future.

2. Determine your goals and objectives once ❏
the fraud has been investigated and
quantified (identify your desired outcomes).

3. Discuss with counsel the potential costs ❏
associated with your desired outcomes to

ensure that the costs of an investigation don't outweigh the potential benefits.

4. Identify an investigation approach and plan. ❑

5. Execute the plan and conduct the   ❑
   investigation, under the direct guidance of
   counsel (and any experts retained by counsel
   on your behalf).

Embezzlement Controls for Business Enterprises

Lester Amos Pratt, CPA

Contents

About the Author   257

Introduction   259

CHAPTER 1   A Fraud Exposure Program   261

CHAPTER 2   To Control Embezzlements of Cash Receipts   265

CHAPTER 3   To Control Embezzlements of Cash
                Disbursements   271

CHAPTER 4   To Control Embezzlements of Merchandise   277

CHAPTER 5   A Control Program for Small Businesses   281

CHAPTER 7   A Checklist of Internal Control Procedures   285

Note: Chapter 6 has been omitted at the request of the Fidelity and Deposit Company of Maryland.

About the Author

Lester A. Pratt is a nationally known specialist in employee fraud investigations. A certified public accountant for 31 years, Mr. Pratt's uncanny instinct for detecting the presence of fraud and trapping its perpetrators has long been made use of by business men, bankers, surety companies and government supervisory agencies.

He has written interestingly on many phases of accounting work and his recent book, *Bank Frauds—Their Detection and Prevention*, was received with wide acclaim in banking circles. Several years ago he also co-authored with Dr. George H. Newlove, of the University of Texas, a two-volume work, *Specialized Accounting*, which is still a college text.

Introduction

No employer likes to consider the possibility that dishonesty on the part of one or more of his employees may some-day cause him a serious loss. Small employers, especially, are inclined to minimize their exposure to losses of this character. Nevertheless, it is a known fact that many thousands of persons in positions of trust and responsibility do "go wrong" every year, often with disastrous results to their employers.

Statistics as to the total annual embezzlement losses in this country are necessarily incomplete because the implications of this crime are such as to cause many of its victims to refrain from publicizing their ill fortune. However, a careful review of all available information on the subject convincingly indicated that stealing by employees is costing American business enter-prises upwards of $500 million a year. This is a staggering tribute to pay to dishonesty and clearly suggests an alarming degree of inefficiency in the average firm's defenses against employee frauds.

This fact stands out: no one has yet discovered a sure-fire method of avoiding the employment of potential embezzlers. Embezzlers follow no pattern, show no recognizable outward signs. They may be 18 or 80, work for a firm four months or forty years, be paid $1,800 or $18,000 and steal anywhere from a few hundred dollars to many hundreds of thousands. For the most part, embezzlements are committed by individuals who have no previous criminal records and whose business and personal backgrounds are beyond reproach.

There are two elements in the crime of embezzlement. One is management's sin; the other is the embezzler's contribution. The first is temptation. If, in the course of his work, an employee is constantly faced with the opportunity to steal, either through inadequate accounting procedures and/or lack of proper internal controls, that's one element. Add to this the second element—and the stage is set for embezzlement.

In addition to providing decent working conditions, reasonable hours, adequate wages and opportunities for advancement, employers have a definite moral obligation to safeguard their employees' integrity by doing everything possible to deter them from yielding to the temptation to take dishonest advantage of their positions. While no system of accounting or internal control has yet been devised that will absolutely prevent embezzlement, nevertheless much can be done to keep an inherently honest individual from misusing his employer's money in a moment of weakness, or under the stress of financial worry. One of the purposes of this treatise is to indicate some of the steps that may be taken to accomplish this worthwhile objective.

CHAPTER 1

A Fraud Exposure Program

A firm's first approach to the problem of controlling dishonesty losses should be to determine the weak links in its defenses against this type of employee fraud. The simplest and easiest way to obtain this needed information is to follow a definite survey program. If such a program is carried out and the results of the survey are acted upon intelligently, the firm's management can rest assured that its exposure to inside thefts has been minimized.

Who should handle the actual work of making the survey? Obviously, he should be someone well-acquainted with the firm's operations. In a small business, the manager or proprietor would be the most logical person. On the other hand, if the business employs well-qualified outside auditors to make semi-annual or annual examinations, the work of making survey should be assigned to them. This task, however, should be treated as a separate assignment, rather than as part of a regular examination, because it is difficult to combine the work of the two investigations due to their different natures.

In any case, such a survey should embrace a thorough investigation of the firm's employment practices, as well as its methods of handling its receipts and disbursements, collections of accounts receivable, customers' accounts, credits and rebates, bank deposits, petty cash funds, payroll, checks,

261

inventories, and all other operations wherein dishonesty losses might originate or occur.

The various controls and other safeguards suggested on the following pages are not intended to represent an ideal dishonesty loss prevention program. However, they do represent the fundamentals of such a program and as such are indicative of the points to which particular attention should be paid in making a survey of the character proposed above.

How Employees Steal

The ways in which employees may misappropriate money or other property of their employers are limited only by their ingenuity. Such thefts may range from the single pocketing of an expensive tool to the most intricate accounting manipulation. Following are some of the more common methods of embezzling money:

1. Issuance of checks in payment of bills of fictitious suppliers and cashing them through a dummy, or by faked endorsement.
2. Invoicing goods below established prices and getting cash "kick-backs" from the purchasers.
3. Raising the amounts of checks, invoices and vouchers after they have been officially approved.
4. Issuing and cashing checks for returned purchases not actually returned.
5. Pocketing the proceeds of cash sales and not recording the transactions.
6. Pocketing collections made on presumably uncollectible accounts.
7. "Lapping" (i.e., pocketing small amounts from incoming payments and applying subsequent remittances on other items to cover the shortages).

8. Forging checks and destroying them when returned by the bank, then concealing the transactions by forcing footings in the cash books or by raising the amounts of legitimate checks.

9. Charging customers more than the duplicate sales slips show and pocketing the difference.

10. Padding payrolls as to rates, time, production or number of employees.

11. Failing to record returned purchases, allowances and discounts and appropriating equivalent amounts of cash.

12. Paying creditors' invoices twice and appropriating the second check.

13. Appropriating checks made payable to "cash" or bank, supposedly for creditors' accounts, payment of notes or other expenses.

14. Stealing from the cash register and tampering with the tape.

15. Misappropriating cash and charging the amounts taken to fictitious customers' accounts.

16. Increasing the amounts of creditors' invoices and pocketing the excess or splitting with the creditors.

17. Pocketing unclaimed wages or dividends.

18. Pocketing portions of collections made from customers and offsetting them on the books by improper credits for allowances of discounts.

CHAPTER 2

To Control Embezzlements of Cash Receipts

Cash receipts require the fullest possible measure of control. Misappropriations of such receipts may be accomplished either before or after they have been recorded. Generally speaking, it is easier to detect an embezzlement of cash if some record of its receipt exists. Consequently, in carrying out a fraud exposure survey, special attention should be paid to the precautions employed to prevent thefts of unrecorded cash receipts, such as cash sales and collections on customers' accounts.

Cash Sales

Cash registers, pre-numbered sales tickets in pad or book form and autographic registers are the three most common safeguards employed in the handling of over-the-counter receipts.

If cash registers are used, each sales clerk preferably should be assigned his own machine and twice a day each register should be cleared by a responsible officer of all cash above a set amount required for making change. Sales clerks should never be permitted to have access to the keys to the locking mechanisms of their registers.

If pre-numbered sales tickets are used, they should be made out in duplicate or triplicate and each sales person should be held accountable for each ticket in his pad or book. At the close of each day, the total of the amounts indicated on the sales tickets should balance with the total amount of cash received by the cashier. To avoid falsification of the sales tickets, at the time of making each sale, both the original and duplicate tickets should be sent to the cashier to be stamped "Paid."

There are a number of autographic registers, or sales-receipting machines, on the market. In general, such devices involve the use of pre-numbered sales tickets which are turned out by a crank, each revolution depositing a copy of the filled-out ticket in a locked compartment. These copies should be removed and checked daily by a responsible official with the amount of cash received by the cashier.

Cash Receipts

The receiving, opening and distribution of incoming mail should be handled by, or under the supervision of, a responsible official other than the cashier or bookkeeper. This person should make a list of all receipts, both cash and checks, showing from whom received, amounts, etc. This list preferably should be made in duplicate on numbered forms, both copies being signed by the person opening the mail and by the cashier to whom the receipts are delivered. The original is retained by the cashier and the duplicate is sent to the auditing or accounting department for filing.

To prevent falsification of cash book entries, each day's list of incoming receipts should be carefully checked against such entries to make sure that they agree.

Because embezzlements of cash often are concealed by underfooting the cash receipts book totals, these footings should be verified at least weekly.

All incoming remittances and other cash receipts should be deposited in the bank intact and each day's receipts should agree with the daily deposits.

All checks received should be stamped "for deposit only" and deposited within 24 hours after they are received.

Bank deposits should be accompanied by three deposit slips, one of which should be stamped by the bank and immediately returned to the person making the deposit for subsequent delivery to the cashier. The other should be mailed by the bank directly to the depositor's auditing department. The third copy is retained by the bank for its record of the deposit.

Each day's deposit slips should be checked against the day's list of remittances and cash receipts.

Bank statements should be received and reconciled by someone other than the person who is in charge of accounting for the firm's receipts and disbursements. All cancelled checks should be carefully examined for possible evidence of alteration, as well as to make sure they have been properly endorsed by the payees. If any errors, erasures or alterations appear on the statement, the bank should be asked to furnish a duplicate.

Unless absolutely unavoidable, the duties of cashier and bookkeeper should be divided between two people, neither of whom should be permitted access to the other's records.

Proceeds from the sale of waste paper, scrap and similar items may amount to a considerable sum in the course of a year and should be carefully watched since such sales are usually made on a bargaining basis and for cash.

Other Good Accounting Practices

All non-cash entries covering allowances, bad debts, discounts, returns, etc. should be made, or at least approved, by a responsible official other than the cashier or bookkeeper.

Before charging off an account as uncollectible, a check should be made to determine whether or not the customer in question actually exists. All accounts regarded as collectible should be transferred to a memorandum control account and periodically reviewed, because subsequent collections on such accounts often add up to sizable amounts.

Accounts receivable should be sampled, or test-checked, from time to time by having some person other than the ledger clerk prepare and mail statements to all such accounts.

Employees who handle credit memos and other adjustments with customers should not be permitted access to the customer's accounts receivable records.

Where the size of the organization permits, another desirable safeguard is to require the ledger clerk in the credit and collection department to switch positions every now and then.

Customers' unpaid balances should be checked at least once a year. These verification reports should be personally mailed and received by the auditor, or by a responsible official. If any customers fail to acknowledge or return these reports, an investigation should be made to determine if such firms or individuals actually exist.

Bookkeepers should not be permitted to make adjustments to bring customers' ledgers into balance with the general ledger account.

Entries in the cash book should be made by someone other than the person who reconciles the bank account, or who checks the cash on hand.

Payments on notes receivable should be received by one person and entered by another.

Periodic Examinations

The importance of having periodic examinations made by competent outside certified public accountants cannot be overemphasized. These audits should be made at least annually and should include an examination of inventory schedules as to price, extensions, footings and such further tests as the situation may require. The audit program also should cover a comprehensive examination and verification of all assets, liabilities, net worth, income and expense accounts. Occasional surprise audits also are highly desirable.

CHAPTER 3

To Control Embezzlements of Cash Disbursements

Effective internal control of the disbursement of funds is somewhat simpler than for cash receipts.

All disbursements, except from a "petty cash fund," should be made by check.

All checks issued should be serially numbered and written either on a check-writing machine or in permanent ink on safety paper.

Countersignatures are desirable, with authority to sign or countersign being delegated to not more than two responsible officials.

If an error is made in writing a check, the check should be voided and another issued.

Cash disbursement records should be independently footed and checked to the related general ledger control accounts.

Petty Cash Fund

Control of this money should begin with the establishment of a specific fund sufficient to meet the daily requirements of the business and this amount should be entered in the general ledger.

No disbursements should be made from this fund without supporting vouchers, signed by the persons receiving the cash and approved by someone in authority. To prevent alteration, these vouchers preferably should be typewritten, or made out in ink or indelible pencil and the amount written out in full (i.e., ten dollars, not $10.00).

Wherever possible, original invoices of vendors should be attached to the petty cash vouchers supporting such disbursements.

The fund should be replenished from time to time by drawing a check in the amount of the paid vouchers in the drawer. At that time, someone other than the employee in charge of the fund should inspect the vouchers for possible evidence of fraud and they should be cancelled by perforation, date stamp, or in some other satisfactory manner so as to prevent their possible re-use.

Frequent unannounced inspections of the vouchers in the petty cash drawer should be made by a responsible official and the fund balanced. This procedure will have the effect of minimizing the risk of petty embezzlements and do much to prevent employees from obtaining unauthorized cash advances.

As a guard against the possibility of an employee increasing the amount of an invoice after its payment, then entering the increased figure on the books and pocketing the difference from miscellaneous cash, all paid purchase invoices should be checked from time to time to make sure that the totals have not been altered.

Cash receipts should never be mingled with petty cash funds.

Purchasing

Wherever the size of the organization permits, the purchasing of all merchandise, either for re-sale or for use in a store or plant, should be centralized. Pre-numbered requisitions should be used to originate the purchasing activity. These should be prepared in triplicate, the original going to the vendor, the duplicate retained in the unfilled order file and the triplicate sent to the receiving clerk. In preparing the latter copy, a short carbon should be used so that the quantity ordered is left blank, making it subsequently necessary for the receiving clerk to insert the quantity actually received.

When the triplicate copy is received by the person in charge of purchasing, the quantity of merchandise or materials indicated is checked with the vendor's invoice and attached to it. The duplicate copy is then taken from the unfilled order file, checked as to price and extensions with the vendor's invoice and filed in the filled-orders file for future reference. The vendor's invoice then is ready for official approval for entry in the firm's accounting records and subsequent payment.

Checks issued in payment of purchases should be accompanied by the applicable purchase invoice and the latter should be initialed by both the person signing the checks and by the countersigner.

Wherever possible, purchasing and receiving functions should be kept entirely separate, so as to minimize the risk of collusion between a vendor and the purchasing agent, to guard against short shipments of merchandise, and, in general, to hold the receiving clerk accountable for all merchandise delivered by the vendor.

Further protection is obtained when a third person (the manager, proprietor, or some other responsible official) takes an active interest in checking purchase invoices for prices, description of goods purchased, quality, quantity, extension of costs, footings, discounts, transportation charges, etc. At least a selective test should be made of all invoices relating to purchases of materials in large quantities and money value.

Wherever practical, competitive bids should be required for the purchase of large quantities of goods to guard against a vendor being given orders at an excessive price, or for inferior quality, with a subsequent cash "kick-back" to the person in charge of purchasing.

When vendors' invoices are paid, they should be stamped "Paid" and both the check numbers and dates of payment noted on the invoices.

Where accommodation purchases are made for the benefit of employees, management should make sure that payment for such items is collected from the employees, either by payroll deductions or cash, and not charged to some expense account.

In the case of purchases made on behalf of customers, with delivery to be made direct by the vendors to the customers, certain safeguards also are necessary to make sure that such orders are properly accounted for and billed to the customers. It usually will suffice in such cases to make a notation on the vendor's invoice to show that the customer has been billed, as well as the date and number of the bill. There have been many cases where a bookkeeper or other clerical employee has deliberately failed to bill a customer in return for a cash "kick-back" from the latter.

Returned purchases may be adequately safeguarded by putting into reverse the system previously suggested with respect to the purchase of merchandise or materials for use in the plant or store.

Many large losses have been caused through duplicate payment of creditors' invoices. In most such cases, the defaulter will select invoices which were paid in previous years and only change the year date. After the check in payment of the falsified invoice has been signed, the defaulter will either forge the endorsement, or perhaps be in collusion with the payee to collect the proceeds of the check. Consequently, creditors' invoices should always be carefully checked before payment to make sure that they have not been falsified in any way.

Payrolls

Where it is practicable to do so, employees should be paid by checks, preferably of a different color than those used for other purposes. It also is desirable that a statement of each employee's earnings and applicable deductions appear on a perforated extension of the check form.

Where employees are paid by cash and a large number of individuals are involved, it is preferable for the employer to arrange with his bank to prepare the payroll.

Current cash receipts should never be used for payroll purposes.

Wherever possible, the preparation of the payroll and paying off of employees should be handled by two different employees, especially if the employees are paid in cash.

If a separate bank account is used for payroll purposes only, the bank statement and cancelled payroll checks should be sent for reconciliation direct to a principal administrative employee who does not participate in the actual preparation of the payroll.

After an appropriate interval—a week is usual—all unclaimed pay should be turned back to the treasurer or other similar official for re-deposit in the bank. It is highly important that unclaimed pay be investigated to disclose any irregularities that may exist as the result of "payroll padding."

Time cards which show erasures of dates should be carefully checked as a guard against the re-use of previously honored cards.

In firms large enough to be departmentalized, the payroll should be supported by time sheets by the department heads. These should be made subject to verification by persons not members of the departments concerned.

The timekeeper who checks employees in at a plant in the morning should not also check them out at night.

Rates of pay, time worked and computations of amounts earned should be reviewed independently at selected intervals. Surprise examinations are the most effective.

Administrative officials should examine any abnormal increase in the number of employees, rates and labor costs.

Officials should not sign payroll checks in blank for emergency use during their absence.

All payroll checks voided for any reason should be retained for examination and audit. They should be mutilated and the signatures torn off so that they cannot be used.

Payroll time cards also should be cancelled in such a way as to prevent their possible re-use.

When a new employee is hired, the employment office or personnel department, as the case may be, should immediately furnish the payroll division with the employee's name, address, title, salary, etc., and this notification should be signed by a responsible officer. To prevent "payroll padding," the same procedure also should be followed when an employee leaves the company.

From time to time, the payroll should be checked to make sure that the number of names corresponds to the number of employees.

CHAPTER 4

To Control Embezzlements of Merchandise

In most cases, embezzlements of merchandise are made possible by the lack of proper controls over the following operations: (1) receiving, (2) delivery and (3) inventory.

Receiving

Wherever possible, the duties of receiving, storekeeping and delivery should be handled by three different individuals.

Generally speaking, controlling the receipt of merchandise or materials is accomplished in the same manner previously described under "Purchasing." Having acknowledged receipt of the goods on the triplicate copy of the purchase order, the receiving clerk then is charged with the custodianship of the property, unless he discharges his responsibility in this respect by delivery of the goods to a storekeeper.

The same procedure should be followed with respect to transfers of merchandise from stockrooms to sales departments. Here again pre-numbered vouchers or requisitions should be used, receipted by the sales clerks and the transfers entered on the inventory records. If the stock numbers are indicated on the sales slips, a perpetual inventory of merchandise in each sales unit can be maintained.

Similar controls over work in process or material sent to jobs away from the plant may be adopted by means of pre-numbered job requisitions.

Where all three duties—receiving, storekeeping and delivery—are performed by a single employee, a perpetual inventory should be maintained by some other clerical employee. In no case should the person in charge of the stockroom also be in charge of the perpetual inventory records.

Acknowledging receipt of merchandise is by no means a "cure-all" in preventing embezzlements of incoming goods. Frequent physical inspections or test-checks of the storeroom to verify the quantity of merchandise on hand should be made by someone other than the person in charge of receiving, storing and delivery of the materials.

Delivery

Controlling the delivery of merchandise to customers is a problem that affects both large and small firms. Both internal and external controls are necessary to curtail losses arising out of this operation. In most cases, such losses are collusive frauds, one or more confederates participating with the defaulter.

Inside employees usually have the best opportunities for initiating this type of theft. For example, an inside employee of a wholesale meat company, who had access to the refrigerator, would arrange to place quantities of meat on a driver's truck in excess of the amount required for deliveries to the firm's regular customers. The driver would sell this extra meat for cash to various markets and split the proceeds with his accomplice. Discovery of the thefts came about only as the result of a tip by a discharged employee.

Rotation of the employees who loaded the meat trucks, or careful spot checking at irregular intervals, would have quickly brought this condition to light and stopped further losses.

In the case of merchandise sold and shipped to customers, satisfactory control usually can be accomplished by the use of pre-numbered shipping tickets, signed or initialed by the shipping clerk at the time the goods are shipped and then sent to the accounting department for entry on the sales and inventory records. The shipping tickets should list all the items to be included in the shipment.

Inventory

Inventories are customarily taken at monthly, semi-annual, or annual intervals, depending upon the size and type of business concerned. Where perpetual inventory records are maintained by someone outside of the storekeeping department, it is possible to exercise effective control over withdrawals or merchandise from the stockroom through the use of pre-numbered requisitions prepared in duplicate. A selective physical count of certain items in stock can then be made on a weekly or monthly basis and compared with the balance shown on the inventory record cards. Any differences should be carefully checked to determine the cause.

In the taking of a physical inventory, sale clerks should inventory merchandise in departments other than the ones where they are regularly employed and persons from departments other than the stockroom should be used in taking the physical inventory of that division. Physical inventories should be made entirely independent of the perpetual inventory records, and the results of each such inventory should be checked with the perpetual inventory by a responsible officer.

Failure to properly control the activities of porters, messengers, charwomen, janitors and other similar employees may lead to large inventory losses. For example, a porter employed by a wholesale liquor dealer made a practice of filling old cartons and trash containers with pint bottles of whiskey. An accomplice, driving what purported to be an ice truck, picked up the loot after hours and delivered it to a certain grocery store. The confederates split the proceeds, which amounted to $35 for each, cash, delivered.

In another case, a porter for a wholesale tobacco dealer after hours would drop cases of cigarettes and cigars out of the storeroom windows to confederates in the alley below, who would dispose of them to various small merchants in the neighborhood. This loss amounted to approximately $65,000 over a period of three years.

The proper control of inventories, with frequent surprise spot checks of merchandise, coupled with storerooms provided with protected windows and doors, will ordinarily prevent losses of this character.

CHAPTER 5

A Control Program for Small Businesses

Many retail firms employ only one office clerk who combines all the various functions of bookkeeping with the collections and disbursement of funds and the custody of various assets. This also is true of many small manufacturing plants whose entire office force may consist of no more than two or three persons.

Since internal control requires the employment of enough people to permit the work to be divided in such a manner as to afford little opportunity for inside thievery without collusion, it is obvious that some other plan must be utilized in firms of the type indicated above to control both honest and dishonest mistakes. The most practical method calls for the proprietor or manager to assume some of the duties of an internal auditor, such as security of transactions, confirmation of items and investigation of original documents and the amounts and entries which result from them.

Where a manager or owner of a small business employs only a bookkeeper, it is possible to institute a program of internal audit to compensate for the lack of internal control. Such a program would embrace the following procedures:

1. All cash receipts should be deposited intact daily.
2. All disbursements should be made by check, countersigned by the manager or proprietor, except small disbursements as are made from a petty cash fund.
3. Bank accounts should be reconciled by the manager or owner each month.
4. Occasionally, outgoing customers' statements should be verified with the accounts receivable ledger and mailed by the manager or owner.
5. The manager or owner should receive and open the mail, particularly during the first few days of each month.
6. The manager or owner should compare all cash receipts with his books and the deposits shown on the bank statement.
7. Receiving and shipping of merchandise should be done by someone other than the bookkeeper and carefully checked by the manager.
8. All journal entries should receive the approval of the manager or owner, especially those having to do with returned sales, allowances and bad debt.
9. The bookkeeper should be bonded for an appropriate amount.

Frequently, the head of a small business will claim that he does carry out such a program. While he may be honest in his opinion, it has been observed in many instances that his failure to understand the principles of responsibility and accountability has resulted in his not checking some significant step, thus leaving the way wide open for embezzlement.

On other occasions, the manager or owner of such a business will claim that he makes regular tests or surprise audits of various accounting phases. It is true, of course, that a systematic program of surprise tests may represent an effective form of internal control or audit, particularly in a small organization. But for such a program to be effective it must first of all be a *program*. Secondly, it must be operated on a predetermined plan in order that the element of surprise actually may be present. If the manager actually does maintain a written program against which he has recorded the dates of his various tests, then his claim may appear credible. Unfortunately, many businessmen think that they are vigilant when, as a matter of fact, they have been lulled into complacency and trustfulness.

The head of every business organization with an office force of only one or two "trusted employees" should remember these conditions present a most fertile field for small embezzlements, and until he has satisfied himself that the internal audit has actually been of such a character as to remedy the deficiencies in internal control, he should carry out the program previously outlined.

CHAPTER 7

A Checklist of Internal Control Procedures

C an you answer "Yes" to these questions?

Cash Receipts

Mail Receipts

1. Is mail opened by a trusted employee other than the cashier or accounts receivable bookkeeper?
2. Is a list of all mail receipts, classified as to checks, cash, money orders, stamps, etc., prepared by person opening mail?
3. Is such a list compared regularly with the cash receipts book?

Other Receipts

1. Are other cash receipts recorded on cash registers or other registering devices so that customers have opportunity to verify?

Note: Chapter 6 has been omitted at the request of the Fidelity and Deposit Company of Maryland.

2. Are totals which have been accumulating in the cash registers or other registering devices locked in and later checked by some other person?
3. If other registering devices are used, are all receipts or tickets pre-numbered?
4. Are unused receipt books or tickets controlled and are all numbers accounted for as receipts of tickets are used or spoiled?
5. Are proceeds from sales of scrap, salvage, etc., safeguarded?
6. Are interest, rent and other periodic revenues recorded so that non-receipt would be investigated?

All Receipts

1. Are deposits made daily of each day's receipts intact and is responsibility fixed until deposit is received by bank?
2. Are all shortages and overages promptly recorded and reported to proper authority?
3. Does someone other than cashier or accounts receivable bookkeeper directly receive bank debit advices (N.S.F. checks, etc.)?
4. Are duties of cashier and accounts receivable bookkeeper and general bookkeeper performed by different persons?
5. Is cash physically safeguarded?
6. Is a detailed record of negotiable notes and securities maintained by the general bookkeeper and the actual documents held by another and are comparisons periodically made by responsible persons?
7. Are totals of cash receipts journals periodically verified and compared to general books by persons other than cashier, accounts receivable bookkeeper, or person keeping general books?

Cash Disbursements

Petty Cash Disbursements

1. Is a specific cash fund maintained for all small disbursements requiring currency?
2. Is the fund of a type wherein the cash and paid tickets at all times equal a constant amount?
3. When the petty cash fund is reimbursed, are all supporting vouchers examined and cancelled by authorized person signing the reimbursement check?
4. Are all petty cash receipts in ink, signed by party receiving money, and dated?
5. Are original invoices obtained wherever possible?
6. Are frequent unannounced inspections made of petty cash fund by someone other than the custodian?

Disbursements by Checks

1. Are all checks on safety paper, serially pre-numbered and all numbers accounted for (including voided checks)?
2. Are all checks written in permanent ink or by check writing machine?
3. At time of signing, are checks completed except for signatures and accompanied by supporting documents on which the check number and payment date appear in ink?
4. Are totals of cash disbursements journals periodically verified and compared to general books by persons other than cashier, accounts receivable bookkeeper, or person keeping general books?
5. Are payrolls paid by check?
6. Are pay rates, time worked and calculations reviewed independently by unannounced examinations?

7. Is actual distribution of pay to employees occasionally supervised with special investigation of unclaimed wages?
8. Is the practice of drawing checks to cash and of signing checks in advance prohibited?

Merchandise

1. Are all purchases authorized by a responsible party?
2. Are all purchase invoices approved for payment only upon evidence of receipt of merchandise?
3. Is proof of receipt of merchandise in written form and numerically controlled?
4. Are purchasing, receiving, and store room functions performed by different individuals who are held accountable for shortages and overages?
5. Are purchases and sales invoices checked for the following: (a) Quantity received and shipped; (b) Quality; (c) Prices; (d) Terms; (e) Shipping charges; (f) Additions and Extensions; (g) Dates (on purchase invoices to prevent re-use or alterations)?
6. Are all accommodation purchases for employees or others properly billed?
7. Are all issues of merchandise (including return purchases) based on written authorization and properly accounted for?
8. Are all issues of merchandise which represent sales invoiced, with special attention to C.O.D.s?
9. Are selling prices clearly set, with any exceptions to standard prices requiring special authorization?
10. Are all return sales replaced in stock and credits therefore approved by a responsible person?
11. If perpetual inventories are maintained, are periodic unannounced counts made by employees other than stock keepers and those preparing the perpetual inventory records?

12. Is responsibility for shortages or overages of inventory fixed and are all adjustments for inventory differences approved by responsible persons?

Bank Statements and Cancelled Checks

1. Are monthly bank statements and cancelled checks received and reconciled to general books by persons other than those who keep the cash records?
2. Are signatures and endorsements on cancelled checks examined, and are checks returned to bank where necessary?
3. Are deposit dates as shown on the bank statement compared to deposit dates as shown by records of cash receipts?

Accounts and Notes Receivable

1. Are allowances for discounts contrary to terms of sale approved by responsible officials?
2. Are all credits to accounts other than those arising out of cash remittances and cash discounts approved by persons in authority other than cashier or accounts receivable bookkeeper?
3. Are write-offs of bad debts authorized by responsible persons?
4. Are records of bad debts which are less than three years old under control?
5. Are customer statements which agree with accounts receivable records mailed at least one time each year with mailing under control of some party other than cashier or accounts receivable bookkeeper?
6. If customers take exceptions to statements, or if statements are returned due to incorrect addresses, are such exceptions communicated directly to authorized persons other than cashier or accounts receivable bookkeeper?

General

1. Are all employees who handle cash, securities, and other valuables bonded in sufficient amount?
2. Are insurance and fidelity bond coverages under the supervision of persons in authority?
3. Are all employees required to take vacations at which time their duties are performed by other employees?
4. Are accounting methods and routines stated in manuals?
5. Are all important records physically safeguarded?

Who Was Lester Amos Pratt?

In becoming a Certified Fraud Examiner, I was required to relearn the field of criminology, which included studying the experts who made fraud and forensic accounting known throughout the years.

Although I have never met many of the well-known experts in this field, I have had the opportunity to meet several nationally recognized experts, many of whom have written books that help fill my fraud library. Those who know me personally know that I have a passion for this field, studying and learning the latest techniques and schemes and writing books to pass along my experience and the things I have learned along the way. In looking back at my experiences and training, I believe I have become pretty knowledgeable in the field of forensic accounting, at least within the context of employee thefts and embezzlement. In all the other areas, I have a general understanding with varying degrees of knowledge and experience.

Prior to blindly purchasing Lester Pratt's book *Embezzlement Controls for Business Enterprises* in 2007 through an online used book auction, I had never even heard of Mr. Pratt. I wasn't sure what I had purchased, but for the price, how could I have gone wrong? When it arrived, I found it wasn't anything I thought it would be. I expected a college-style textbook, and instead I received a 31-page brochure-style book. No frills, no fancy graphics on the cover, and no hard cover. Perhaps life was simpler in 1952 when Mr. Pratt wrote it, focused more on content than on looks and eye appeal. I breezed through the first time reading all 31 pages, and then went back to reread each section, realizing that Mr. Pratt had captured in 31 pages what others have set out to accomplish in hundreds of pages. Thirty-one pages, direct on point, telling readers exactly what they needed to do to address the problem of employee theft, written in 1952. The book even provides a picture of Mr. Pratt, sitting at his desk, holding a pipe, just as one would expect to find him, as a forensic accountant, in 1952.

Once I realized the find that I had stumbled on, I set out on what has been a two-year journey to learn as much about Mr. Pratt as possible. I only wish he were still alive so that I could have interviewed him. I am sure he would have been a treasure trove of knowledge, experience, and stories about the fraud cases he completed. In my quest to find more about Mr. Pratt, I searched the nation for any relatives who could tell me more about him and his accomplishments.

Unfortunately, to date I have been unsuccessful in locating any of Mr. Pratt's relatives. I have found families of two other individuals named Lester A. Pratt, one who was from Rhode Island and the other from New Hampshire. The problem is neither was Lester A. Pratt, fraud examiner and forensic accountant.

I would love to hear from anyone with information about Mr. Pratt, especially any relatives who could shed more light on him and his accomplishments. I can be reached at steve@ForensicAccountingServices.com.

I would like to provide a special thank-you to everyone who helped me search for information about Mr. Pratt. Here is what I have learned to date about Lester Amos Pratt, nationally recognized expert in the field of employee embezzlement and bank fraud:

- Born in 1892
- Enlisted in the United States Army on November 10, 1917
- Elected Accountant, Compensation Board, Navy Department, December 9, 1919
- Licensed as a Certified Public Accountant in North Carolina in 1920
- Coauthored *Industrial Accounting: CPA with Questions and Problems* in 1921
- Coauthored *Specialized Accounting* in 1925
- Authored *Bank Directors Held Liable for Loss by Embezzlement* in 1940
- Referenced in the July 21, 1947, issue of *Time* magazine, "Withdrawals. In Manhattan, CPA Lester A. Pratt, a serious student, divulged that 1) there are 210 ways to crack a bank without gun or dynamite, 2) bank officials and the help get away with $2 and $6 million a year, and 3) 65% soon get caught—if they keep on working the same bank."
- Authored *I Catch Bank Embezzlers* in 1948
- Authored *Fraud Prevention Program for the Small Bank* in 1949
- Authored *Bank Frauds: Their Detection and Prevention* in 1950
- Authored *Connecticut Trust Conference: Directors' Examinations of Trusts* in 1951
- Authored *Embezzlement Controls for Business Enterprises* in 1952
- Authored *Still Better Audit Control* in 1952
- Authored *Audit Control of Bank Operations* in 1952
- Authored *Embezzlement Controls and other Safeguards for Banks* in 1958

- Authored *The "Whole" Story of American Bank Checks and Their Effect on Banking* in 1958
- Authored *The Responsibilities of Bank Directors* in 1961
- Authored *Bank Frauds: Their Detection and Prevention, 2nd Edition* in 1965

About the Author

Stephen Pedneault, CPA/CFF, CFE, is the principal of Forensic Accounting Services, LLC, a CPA firm in Glastonbury, Connecticut specializing in forensic accounting, employee fraud, and litigation support matters. His technical expertise and intuitive investigative awareness have garnered him the respect of the legal, accounting, and law enforcement communities. As a result, Steve is called upon as a litigation expert on an ongoing basis and is considered a highly regarded member of legal teams.

Working in public accounting for over 22 years, Steve is a Certified Public Accountant (CPA), a Certified Fraud Examiner (CFE), and Certified in Financial Forensics (CFF). He has an associate's degree in criminal justice from Manchester Community College and a bachelor's degree in accounting from Eastern Connecticut State University, where he graduated summa cum laude.

Steve's first book, *Fraud 101*, was published by John Wiley & Sons, Inc. in September 2009. His second book, *Anatomy of a Fraud Investigation* (also published by Wiley) was released in January 2010. *Preventing and Detecting Employee Embezzlement: A Practical Guide* (Wiley) is Steve's third book in less than a year. Steve has authored numerous articles that have appeared in local and national publications. Business and student organizations request him to speak on a wide variety of subjects, including forensic accounting, fraud prevention, risk assessment, embezzlement, probate concerns, business valuation, and other related topics on an ongoing basis. He is often referenced and quoted in articles appearing locally, regionally, and nationally.

Through his investigative work, Steve has examined frauds ranging from a few thousand dollars to amounts well in excess of $5 million. His expertise also lies in preventing and investigating embezzlements and financial statement frauds, evaluating financial disclosures in matrimonial and probate concerns, as well as other types of forensic accounting matters.

As an adjunct professor to the University of Connecticut faculty, Steve has authored an innovative course on forensic accounting that has been used since 2008 as an online class within UConn's Masters of Science in Accounting (MSA) program. The course provides an overview of forensic accounting, identifying the qualities and attributes required of a forensic accountant, and provides students with an approach and skill set to enable them to perform a forensic accounting assignment.

Index

A

Acceptance stage of grieving
    process, 20, 21, 23
Access control. *See also*
    Passwords; User IDs
    accounting systems, 206, 207,
      211–216
    bank statements, 81, 173. *See*
      also Electronic banking
    bookkeeping, 206, 207,
      209
    checks, 81–84, 206, 210
    electronic banking, 98,
      124–127, 132
    inventory, 154, 156, 157
    office supplies, parts, and
      materials, 166
    and opportunity, 45
    payroll records, 206, 207
    petty cash, 86
Accountants
    Embezzlement Controls for
      Business Enterprises (Pratt,
      1952), 268, 269

financial reports, review of,
    195, 197
    forensic, 245, 246
    relationship with, 239
    use of, 196, 197, 200, 202, 203,
      222
Accounting systems. *See also*
    Bookkeeping
    access control, 206, 207,
      211–216
    and accountants, role of, 197,
      222
    audit logs, 213, 214, 222, 223,
      226
    backups, 211, 216–220
    and bank reconciliations, 181,
      182
    check generation, 80–83
    integrated, 205, 206, 208
    inventory, 161
    proprietary information,
      protection of, 211, 220–222
    purchasing and cash
      disbursements, 71
    risks, 210

Accounting systems *(continued)*
software, 205, 206. *See also*
QuickBooks
Accounts payable, 77, 84–86,
89, 194, 196.
See also Payments
Accounts receivable
controls, 39–41, 44–46, 52, 53,
55, 57, 194, 196
*Embezzlement Controls for
Business Enterprises* (Pratt,
1952), 261, 268, 282, 285
Adjustments to customer
accounts
controls, 48–51
*Embezzlement Controls for
Business Enterprises* (Pratt,
1952), 262, 263, 267, 268,
274, 282, 288, 289
Alarm systems, 140, 141, 156,
170
Anger, 20–23
Anti-fraud triangle, 223, 227
Applications. *See* Job applications
Approvals
debit memos and adjustments,
48, 57
expense reimbursements,
104–109, 112, 113
payroll package and reports,
149
purchasing, 76–78, 88
refunds and returns, 35, 38, 54
ATMs (automated teller
machines), 45, 51, 121, 122,
128, 129, 180, 181
Attorneys
and discovery of theft or
embezzlement, advice on,
240–247
hiring practices, legal advice
on, 1, 3, 4
insurance claims, legal
assistance with, 231–233
relationship with, 239
Audit logs, 213, 214, 222, 223,
226

B

Background checks, 11–13
Backups, 211, 216–220
Bad debts, *Embezzlement
Controls for Business
Enterprises* (Pratt, 1952),
267, 268, 282, 289
Balance sheet, 194
Bank deposits, 46, 115, 116, 120.
See also Electronic banking
Banks and banking
bankers, relationship with, 239
banks and bank accounts,
changing, 121, 122
electronic banking. *See*
Electronic banking
lockbox services, 44, 45, 129
online, 122, 123
Patriot Act, 121
traditional banking, 115–117
Bank statements. *See also*
Checks; Electronic banking
access to, 81, 173
case studies, 174–177, 183–185
check images, 178, 179, 181
checklist, 187, 188
and checks paid to fictitious
vendors, 72–75
*Embezzlement Controls for
Business Enterprises* (Pratt,
1952), 267, 275, 282, 289
monitoring, 127, 129–131,
133–135, 173, 177, 178, 187
outstanding checks, 183
reconciliations, 181–184, 188

Bargaining, 20, 22, 23
Behavior as indicator of fraud,
    26, 27
Biometric scanners, 144
Bookkeeping. *See also*
    Accounting systems
    access control, 206, 207, 209
    and accounting system
        integration, 205, 206
    checklist, 224, 225
    manual systems, 206–209,
        224
    outside services, 197
    QuickBooks, 71, 81, 190, 194,
        205, 206, 222, 223, 225, 226
    software systems, 209–222,
        224–226
Business owners
    communication with
        employees, 25, 26, 29
    employees, importance of
        knowing, 25–27. *See also*
        Employees
    employees as family, 19
    grieving process after
        fraud/embezzlement by
        trusted employee, 19–21

C

Case studies
    access control, checks, 83, 84
    adjustments, diverted
        payments concealed
        through, 49–51
    backups, 217–220
    bank deposits, 47, 48
    bank statements, 174–177,
        183–185
    benefits, termination of, 143
    cash registers, 207–209
    checks, altered, 198–200
    client list, poaching by former
        employee, 15, 16
    credit card refunds, 63–66
    debit card misuse, 93, 94
    educational background, 10
    electronic banking, 118, 119,
        122, 123, 130, 131
    employee reaction to
        confrontation, 21, 22
    fictitious vendors, 72–75,
        78–80
    financial reports, 191–193
    insurance claims, 233, 234
    inventory, theft of by
        employees, 154, 155, 158,
        159
    payroll, 145, 146, 148
    proprietary information, theft
        of, 221
    service personnel, work on the
        side, 42, 43
    video surveillance, 163–165
    voided sales, 36, 37
    wrongful accusation, 241, 242
Cash disbursements, 80–84,
    88–89. *See also* Purchasing
    and cash disbursements
    *Embezzlement Controls for
    Business Enterprises* (Pratt,
    1952), 271, 282, 287, 288
Cashiers, 34, 35
Cash receipts. *See* Sales, cash
    receipts, and collections
Cash registers, 207, 208
    *Embezzlement Controls
    for Business Enterprises*
    (Pratt, 1952), 263, 265, 285,
    286
Cash sales. *See* Sales, cash
    receipts, and collections
Cell phones, use of in theft of
    information, 81

Characteristics of embezzlers,
*Embezzlement Controls for
Business Enterprises* (Pratt,
1952), 259, 260
Checklists
accounting systems, 224, 225
bank statements and
reconciliations, 187, 188
bookkeeping, 224–225
credit card, business use of,
99, 100
credit card sales, transactions,
and merchant statements,
69, 70
debit card, business use of, 99,
100
discovery of theft or
embezzlement, 249–251
electronic banking, 132–135
employee expense
reimbursements, 111–113
employees, monitoring and
awareness of, 29, 30
financial reports, 202, 203
hiring practices, 17, 18
insurance, 236, 237
inventory, 169–172
payroll, 151, 152
purchasing, cash
disbursements, and petty
cash, 88–90
sales, cash receipts, and
collections, 54–57
Checks. *See also* Electronic
banking
access control, 81–84, 206, 210
altered, 198–200
automated clearing house
(ACH) conversion, 117, 119
canceled checks, 117, 178,
179, 181, 187
checklist, 88, 89
and diversion of customer
payments, 46
electronic banking processing,
117–119
*Embezzlement Controls for
Business Enterprises* (Pratt,
1952), 262, 263, 267, 271,
273–276, 282, 287–289
fictitious vendors, checks paid
to, 72–75, 77
generating and signing, 77,
80–84
images of, 178, 179, 181
lockboxes, use of, 44, 45, 129
outstanding, 183
signatures, 72, 75, 77, 80–84,
89, 124, 125
and traditional banking, 115,
116
truncated, 117, 118
types of, 82
Cleaning crews, 81, 82, 210
COBRA. *See* Consolidated
Omnibus Budget
Reconciliation Act (COBRA)
COBRA benefits, 141
Collections
accounts receivable, 39–41,
44–46, 52, 53, 55, 57, 194,
196
process, 44–47
Communication with employees,
25, 26, 29
Computers and hard drives. *See
also* Passwords; User IDs
backups, 211, 216–220
check images, storing, 128
computerized bookkeeping
and accounting systems. *See*
Accounting systems

forensic computer specialists,
245, 246, 250
inventory and tracking of, 153,
166, 170
laptops, 166
software. *See* Software
USB ports, 218, 222
virus protection, 215
Confidentiality, company policy
on, 14–15
Consolidated Omnibus Budget
Reconciliation Act (COBRA),
141
Credit cards
business use of, 94–96, 99, 100
checklist for business use of,
99, 100
checklist for sales,
transactions, and merchant
statements, 69, 70
debit cards, compared, 91, 92
liability for fraudulent
transactions, 91, 92
merchant statement, 61, 67, 68,
70
monthly statements, review of,
94–96
refunds and credits, 61–70
sales, 59–61, 69
Credit checks, 4, 5, 13, 14
Credit sales, 39, 40, 55. *See also*
Sales, cash receipts, and
collections
Criminal liability
alternative sentencing, 23
decision to prosecute, 246
law enforcement, notification
of crime, 230, 232–234, 243,
244, 246, 249
prison time, 23
restitution, 23

D

Debit cards
account activity, daily
monitoring of, 98
business use of, 96–98, 100,
101
case study, 93, 94
checklist for business use of,
100, 101
credit cards, compared, 91, 92
and electronic banking, 98
liability for fraudulent
transactions, 92
Debit memos, 48, 51
Denial, 20, 21, 23
Deposit slips, 46. *See also* Bank
deposits
Depression, 20, 23
Desktop deposits, 120, 127, 128.
See also Electronic banking
Detection of employee theft and
embezzlement, 227, 236. *See
also* Discovery of theft or
embezzlement; Policies and
procedures
financial reports, 195, 196
inventory, 166, 167, 171, 172
payroll schemes, 195
purchasing and cash
disbursement schemes, 195
Disaster recovery. *See* Backups
Disbursement cycle. *See*
Purchasing and cash
disbursements
Discovery of theft or
embezzlement
actions requiring legal advice,
243
anger, 20–23
checklist, 249–251

Discovery of theft *(continued)*
  considerations in determining
    course of action, 246, 247
  due diligence, 243–246
  emotional response to, 240
  evidence, 27, 240, 243–246.
    See also Evidence
  forensic accountants, use of,
    245, 246
  forensic computer specialists,
    use of, 245, 246
  grieving process. *See* Grieving
    process and
    fraud/embezzlement by
    trusted employees
  insurance claims. *See*
    Insurance
  legal advice, 240–247
  objectivity, need for, 241, 242,
    245
  professionals, need for
    involvement of, 239
  reaction to, stages of, 21–24
  removal of employee, 244
  termination of employee, 244
  and wrongful accusation, 241,
    242, 245
Documentation
  credit card refunds, 62, 67
  hiring procedure, 3
  payroll, 139, 140
  shredding, 82
Due diligence
  discovery of theft or
    embezzlement, 243–246
  employees, screening, 1, 2,
    5–10, 17
  vendors, 76, 88

E

E-mail
  accounts, closing, 141, 212

  alerts, 38, 163, 167
  attachments, 221, 222
  monitoring, 221, 222, 243
Education, verifying, 9, 10
Electronic banking
  access control, 98, 124–127,
    132
  ATMs, 121, 122, 128, 129
  authority, 124, 125
  bank statements, monitoring,
    127, 129–131, 133–135
  and check processing,
    117–119
  checklist, 132–135
  daily reconciliations, 128, 129,
    135
  and debit card use, 98
  deposits, 120, 127, 128, 134,
    135
  disbursements, 45, 122,
    125–127, 132, 133
  internal controls, 124
  online banking, 122, 123
*Embezzlement Controls for
    Business Enterprises* (Pratt,
    1952)
  about, xiv, 291, 292
  accounts receivable, 261, 268,
    282, 285
  allowances, discounts, and
    returns, 262, 263, 267, 268,
    274, 282, 288, 289
  audits by outside accountants,
    268, 269
  bad debts, 267, 268, 282, 289
  bank statements, 267, 275, 282,
    289
  and basic controls, 173
  cash disbursements, 271, 282,
    287, 288
  cash receipts, 265–267, 285,
    286

cash registers, 263, 265, 285, 286
cash sales, 265
characteristics of embezzlers, 259, 260
checks, 262, 263, 267, 271, 273–276, 282, 287–289
delivery of merchandise, 278, 279
employer's responsibilities, 260
fidelity bonds, 282, 290
insurance, 290
internal audits, 281–283
internal control procedures, checklist, 285–290
inventory, 279, 280, 288, 289
methods of embezzlement, 262, 263
payroll, 275, 276
petty cash, 261, 271, 272, 282, 287
purchasing, 272–275, 288
receiving of merchandise, 277, 278, 288
segregation of duties, 266–268, 272, 278, 279, 282, 285–289
small businesses, 281–283
statistics on embezzlement, 259
surprise audits and examinations, 269, 276, 280, 282, 283
survey of business practices, 261, 262
temptation, 260
Emotional response to discovery, 240. *See also* Grieving process and fraud/ embezzlement by trusted employees
Employee Retirement Income Security Act (ERISA), 228

Employees
adding or changing, 138–143
awareness of fraud by coworker, 26
behavior of and indications of fraud, 26, 27
communication with, 25, 26, 29
credit cards, use of, 95, 96
debit cards, use of, 97
employment eligibility verification (Form I-9), 8, 207
expense reimbursement. *See* Expense reimbursement
fidelity bonds, 228, 282, 290
hiring. *See* Hiring practices
importance of knowing, 24, 25
orientation, 14, 15
payroll. *See* Payroll
reaction after discovery of fraud/embezzlement, stages of, 21–24
reasons for committing fraud/embezzlement, 24
removal of, 244
tax implications of expense reimbursements, 107, 109
termination of, 141, 244
theft by, 153–155, 166, 170, 171. *See also* Inventory
trusted employees, 19–24, 220
wrongful accusation, 241, 242, 245
Employer's responsibilities, *Embezzlement Controls for Business Enterprises* (Pratt, 1952), 260
Encryption, 215
Entitlement, 27

Evidence
  discovery of theft or
    embezzlement, 27, 240,
    243–246
  and electronic banking, 119,
    120
  insurance claims, 235
Expense reimbursement, 103–113

F

Fidelity bonds
  *Embezzlement Controls for
    Business Enterprises* (Pratt,
    1952), 282, 290
  use of, 228
Financial need as element of
    fraud triangle, 24
Financial reports
  and accounting systems, 190,
    193, 194
  and business performance,
    analysis of, 190, 193–195
  case study, 191–193
  checklist, 202, 203
  monthly, 190, 193–195, 201,
    202
  review of, 194–195
  theft and embezzlement,
    detection of, 195, 196
Firewalls, 215
Forensic accountants, 245, 246
Forensic computer specialists,
    245, 246
Forms
  Form I-9, 8, 207
  IRS. *See* Internal Revenue
    Service (IRS)
  payroll, 139, 140, 151
  tracking, 208–210
Fraud investigations, time frame
    for, 20
Fraud triangle, elements of, 24

G

General ledger, 194
Gift cards, 162
Global positioning system (GPS),
    42
Grieving process and
    fraud/embezzlement by
    trusted employees, 19–24

H

Hiring practices
  applications, 3–5, 13
  background checks, 11–13
  case studies, 10, 15, 16
  checklist, 17, 18
  checklists, use of, 140, 141
  confidentiality and proprietary
    information policies,
    14–15
  credit checks, 4, 5, 13, 14
  as defense against
    theft and embezzlement,
    1
  documentation, 3, 4
  due diligence, 1, 2, 5–10
  education, verifying, 9, 10
  employment eligibility
    verification (Form I-9), 8,
    207
  legal advice, need for, 1, 3, 4
  legal restrictions, 1, 2
  orientation, 14
  past employment, verifying, 8,
    9
  personal information,
    verifying, 7, 8
  policies and procedures, 3, 4,
    14, 16
  references, 2, 3, 11
  referrals, 2, 3
  and resume fraud, 6, 7

I

Income statement, 194
Insurance
adequacy of coverage,
230
agent, relationship with,
239
checklist, 236, 237
claims procedure, 230–237,
246
coverage, 228, 236
*Embezzlement Controls for
Business Enterprises* (Pratt,
1952), 290
investigations, 234, 235
losses, calculation of, 229
need for, 227, 228
Internal audits, *Embezzlement
Controls for Business
Enterprises* (Pratt, 1952),
281–283
Internal controls
*Embezzlement Controls for
Business Enterprises* (Pratt,
1952), 285–290
importance of, 27, 28
Internal Revenue Service (IRS)
Form 940, 149
Form 941, 149
Form 1096, 149
Form 1099, 149
Form W-2, 149
Form W-4, 8, 206
meal reimbursements, 108
mileage reimbursement, 107,
109
Inventory
access control, 154, 156, 157
checklist, 169–172
detection techniques, 166, 167,
171, 172

*Embezzlement Controls
for Business Enterprises*
(Pratt, 1952), 279, 280,
288, 289
monthly reports, 194
ordering, 156, 157, 158, 169
receiving, 156, 157, 159, 160,
169
reconciling, 162, 163, 165, 170
recording, 156, 157, 160, 161,
169, 170
retail businesses, 153–165
safeguarding, 156, 157, 161,
162, 170
segregation of duties, 159,
160
supplies, tools, and equipment
for business use, 42, 166,
170, 171
video surveillance, 156, 157,
161–165, 167
Investment accounts, 178
Invoices, review and approval of
for payment, 77. *See also*
Purchasing and cash
disbursements

J

Janitors. *See* Cleaning crews
Job applications. *See also* Hiring
practices
credit checks, 4, 5, 13
false, incomplete, or
misleading information, 4
policies and procedures, need
for, 3, 4
resume fraud, 6, 7
review of by attorney, 3, 4
supporting documentation, 4
verification of information,
5–10

K

Kickbacks, 44

L

Laptops, 166. *See also* Computers
and hard drives
Law enforcement, notification of
crime, 230, 232–234, 243,
244, 246, 249
Legal advice. *See* Attorneys
Lockboxes, use of, 44, 45, 129

M

Manual bookkeeping systems,
206–209, 224. *See also*
Bookkeeping
Meals, reimbursement for, 108
Methods of embezzlement,
*Embezzlement Controls for
Business Enterprises* (Pratt,
1952), 262, 263
Mileage, reimbursement for, 103,
106, 107, 109
Motives for committing fraud, 24
Mystery shoppers, use of, 38

N

Nonaccountable plan, 109
Nonsigning users, 124–125, 127,
132

O

Office supplies, 166, 170, 171
Online banking, 122, 123. *See
also* Electronic banking
Opportunity, 24, 45
Orientation, 14
Outside services, use of, 147, 197
Owners. *See* Business owners

P

P-cards (procurement cards),
103–105, 111
Passwords
for banking systems, 124–125,
132
for computer systems, 83,
211–213, 215, 223
for new employees, 140
for sales systems, 35, 208
Past employment, verifying, 8, 9
Patriot Act, 121
Payments. *See also* Purchasing
and cash disbursements
accounts payable. *See*
Accounts payable
electronic bill payments, 126,
127. *See also* Electronic
banking
employee expense
reimbursements, 109, 110,
113
forms for tracking, 208
Payroll
access control, 206, 207
adding, changing, and
terminating employees,
138–143
approvals, 149
case studies, 145, 146, 148
checklist, 151, 152
checklists, use of, 140, 141, 151
*Embezzlement Controls for
Business Enterprises* (Pratt,
1952), 275, 276
forms, 139, 140, 151, 206, 207
fraud, 141–142, 144–148
outside services, 147
processing, 137, 138, 142–149,
151, 152
schemes, detecting, 195

segregation of duties, 141–142, 147

tax returns, 149, 150, 152

time tracking systems, 142, 144–145

vacation, sick, and personal time, 137, 142, 145

Personal information, verifying, 7, 8

Petty cash

controls, 86, 87, 90

Embezzlement Controls for Business Enterprises (Pratt, 1952), 261, 271, 272, 282, 287

Point-of-sale terminals, 34, 35, 157, 163, 205–206

software, 59

Police. *See* Law enforcement, notification of crime

Policies and procedures

cash drawer, reconciling, 38

checkout areas, 35

checks, generating and signing, 80–84

computer passwords and user IDs, 211, 212. *See also* Passwords; User IDs

confidentiality and proprietary information, 14–16

credit card refunds, 62

credit cards, business use of, 95, 96

debit memos and adjustments, 48

documenting, 3

expense reimbursement, 104–107

hiring practices, 3–5

importance of, 3

inventory, 157

payroll, 139, 140

registers and point-of-sale terminals, 34, 35

Post office boxes, 44–46, 76, 77, 79, 80, 129, 142

Pratt, Lester Amos, xiv, 173, 248, 257, 291–294

Prevention of employee theft and embezzlement, 33, 223, 227, 236. *See also* *Embezzlement Controls for Business Enterprises* (Pratt, 1952); Policies and procedures

Procurement cards (p-cards), 103–105, 111

Proprietary information, 14–16, 81, 211, 220–222

Purchase orders

and accounting systems, 210

and inventory control, 157, 158, 169

purchasing process, 76, 78–80, 88

and service invoices, 41

Purchases, employee

reimbursement for, 103, 108, 109

Purchasing and cash disbursements

accounting systems, 71. *See also* Accounting systems

accounts payable, 77, 84–86, 89

case studies, 72–75, 78–80, 83, 84

cash disbursements, 80–84, 88, 89

checklist, 88–90

checks, generating and signing, 77, 80–84. *See also* Checks

Purchasing and cash
disbursements *(continued)*
*Embezzlement Controls for
Business Enterprises* (Pratt,
1952), 272–275, 288
invoices, review and approval
of for payment, 77
petty cash, 86, 87, 90
purchases, 75–80, 88
schemes, detecting, 195
Purchasing cards (p-cards),
103–105, 111

Q

QuickBooks
benefits of, 81, 194, 206,
222–223
drawbacks of, 71, 190, 206,
222–223
securing, 205, 222–223, 225,
226
used in fraud cases, 79,
175–176

R

Rationalization, as element of
fraud triangle, 24, 25
Receipts
expense reimbursement,
104–109, 112, 113
returned merchandise, 162
Receiving. *See* Shipping and
receiving
Reconciliation
bank deposits, 46–48
bank statements, 181–184,
188
cash drawers, 35, 38, 54
credit card refunds and credits,
63–66, 70
credit card sales, 61, 69

electronic banking, 128, 129,
135
expense reimbursements and
receipts, 104, 105
inventory, 162, 163, 165, 170
office supplies, tools, and
equipment, 166
payments, 44, 46, 57
services, 40, 55
triangular, 46, 47, 61
References, 2, 3, 11
Referrals, 2, 3
Refunds and returns
approvals, 35, 36, 54
*Embezzlement Controls for
Business Enterprises* (Pratt,
1952), 262–263, 267–268,
274, 282, 288, 289
processing, 61–70
receipts, 162
sales, cash receipts, and
collections, 35–38
Remote deposit capture (desktop
deposits), 120, 127, 128
Response to discovery of
identified or potential issue.
See Discovery of theft or
embezzlement
Resume fraud, 6, 7
Retail sales, 32–39. *See also* Sales,
cash receipts, and
collections
Returns. *See* Refunds and returns
Revenue cycle. *See* Sales, cash
receipts, and collections

S

Sales, cash receipts, and
collections
accounts receivable, 39–41,
44–46, 52–53, 55, 57

adjustments to customer
   accounts, 48–51, 55, 57
case studies, 36–37, 42–43,
   47–51
cash receipts cycle, 31
cash registers, 207, 208
cash sales, 33–34
cash skim, 195–196
checklist, 54–57
collections process, 44–47, 56,
   57
credit card sales. *See* Credit
   cards
credit sales, 39, 40, 55
debit memos, 48, 51, 57
*Embezzlement Controls for
   Business Enterprises* (Pratt,
   1952), 265–267, 285, 286
as embezzlement target, 31, 32
importance of, 31
receipts, issuance of, 34
recording and tracking systems
   for sales, 32, 33, 54, 55
retail sales, 32–39, 55
returns and refunds. *See*
   Refunds and returns
services, 33, 40–44, 55, 56
and shipping procedures, 40
Security personnel, 162
Segregation of duties
*Embezzlement Controls for
   Business Enterprises* (Pratt,
   1952), 266–268, 272, 278,
   279, 282, 285–289
inventory control, 159, 160
payroll processing, 138, 139,
   141–143, 147, 152
and small businesses, 52, 138,
   139, 174
Services, 40–44
Shipping and receiving

*Embezzlement Controls for
   Business Enterprises* (Pratt,
   1952), 277, 278, 288
inventory control, 156–162,
   169
shipping procedures, 40
video surveillance, 161, 162
Shoplifting, 153, 162
Sick days, 137, 142, 145
Signatures
   bank signature cards, 124
   credit card purchases, 60
   stamps, 72, 75, 83, 89, 174
Small businesses
   *Embezzlement Controls for
      Business Enterprises* (Pratt,
      1952), 281–283
   and segregation of duties, 52,
      138, 139, 174
Software
   accounting systems, 205, 206.
      See also QuickBooks
   bookkeeping, 209–222,
      224–226
   for monitoring accounting
      system user activity, 214
Surprise audits and examinations,
   *Embezzlement Controls for
      Business Enterprises* (Pratt,
      1952), 269, 276, 280, 282,
      283
Surveillance. *See* Video
   surveillance

T

Tax considerations, employee
   expense reimbursements,
   107, 109
Tax forms. *See* Internal Revenue
   Service (IRS)

Tax returns, payroll, 149, 150, 152
Time tracking systems, 142, 144–145
Tools and equipment, 42, 166, 170, 171
Travel costs, reimbursement for, 103, 107, 108

U

U.S. Citizenship and Immigration Services, Form I-9, 8, 207
USB ports and flash drives, 218, 222
User IDs, 35, 83, 124, 125, 132, 140, 211, 212, 215

V

Vacation time, 26, 27, 137, 142, 145
Vendors, 76–80, 160
Video surveillance

doors, 156, 157
inventory control, 156, 157, 161–165, 167
office areas, 163–165
retail sales, 33, 34, 38, 161, 162
shipping and receiving areas, 161, 162
triggering event, 38, 163, 167
Virus protection, 215
Voids, 35–38. *See also* Refunds and returns
Voids and returns, 35–38. *See also* Refunds and returns

W

Web sites
fakeresume.com, 6
false diplomas, degrees, and transcripts, availability of, 9
judicial system records, 12
Wrongful accusation, 241, 242, 245